BULLIES

BULLIES

A FRIENDSHIP

ALEX ABRAMOVICH

HENRY HOLT AND COMPANY
NEW YORK

Henry Holt and Company, LLC
Publishers since 1866
175 Fifth Avenue
New York, New York 10010
www.henryholt.com

Henry Holt ® and ® are registered trademarks of
Henry Holt and Company, LLC.

Library of Congress Cataloging-in-Publication Data

Names: Abramovich, Alex, 1972–
Title: Bullies : a friendship / Alex Abramovich.
Description: First edition. | New York : Henry Holt and Company, 2016.
Identifiers: LCCN 2015026132| ISBN 9780805094282 (hardback) |
  ISBN 9781429949064 (electronic book)
Subjects: LCSH: Abramovich, Alex, 1972—Friends and associates. | Latham,
  Trevor. | Male friendship—California—Oakland. | Oakland (Calif.)—
  Biography. | Authors, American—California—Oakland—Biography. |
  Motorcyclists—California—Oakland—Biography. | Oakland (Calif.)—Social
  conditions—21st century. | Abramovich, Alex, 1972—Childhood and youth. |
  Bullying—New York (State)—Long Island. | Violence—Psychological aspects. |
  BISAC: BIOGRAPHY & AUTOBIOGRAPHY / Personal Memoirs. |
  BIOGRAPHY & AUTOBIOGRAPHY / Criminals & Outlaws.
Classification: LCC F869.O2 A23 2016 | DDC 979.4/660530922—dc23
LC record available at http://lccn.loc.gov/2015026132

ISBN: 978-0-8050-9428-2

Henry Holt books are available for special promotions and premiums.
For details contact: Director, Special Markets.

First Edition 2016

Designed by Meryl Sussman Levavi

Printed in the United States of America

1 2 3 4 5 6 7 8 9 10

For Lucy

People who are powerless make an open theater of violence.

—DON DELILLO

BULLIES

CHAPTER ONE

The only pictures I tacked up over my desk, or anywhere else in the house during my first year in Oakland, were old black-and-white photographs of Abdo Allen's decommissioned Sherman tank. After a few months, I photocopied three of the photos, folded the copies up, and tucked them into my wallet. That way, if some out-of-town friend were to ask me, "How did Oakland get to be so fucked up?" I could start with some history, show them some pictures.

The question came up a lot that year, which was also the year of Cairo's Tahrir Square and New York's Zuccotti Park, and the first time in decades that Oakland, a working-class city on San Francisco Bay, became a fixture in the national news cycle. It was the year of Occupy Oakland, and the Black Muslim Bakery murder trials, the year that Harold Camping's Oakland-based Family Radio ministry predicted the end of the world, twice, while Oakland's murder rate (already one of the nation's highest) ticked upward, and the year that the *New York Times* picked Oakland to be the world's fifth most desirable place to

1

visit (something about "upscale cocktail bars, turning once-gritty Oakland into an increasingly appealing place to be after dark"), placing it higher on the list than Glasgow, Moscow, and Florence. This was news to the city's residents—though Oakland did have good bars, and the local cops were so overwhelmed that, if you steered clear of the highway patrol, it was almost impossible to get a DUI there. But two days later, the *Times* published a follow-up: "Shootings Soar in Oakland," the headline read. "Children Often the Victims."

"How *did* Oakland get to be so fucked up?"

I'd fumble around for my wallet.

The first photo I'd tucked away there was taken by an AP stringer in the summer of 1960. It showed the tank from behind as it ripped through a house in West Oakland. The second photograph showed the tank from the front, covered in the rubble of a lot it had already cleared. Both photographs looked like they could have belonged in a History Channel documentary about World War II. But the third photograph showed the tank in full profile. You could see the words "ABDO S. ALLEN Co." hand-painted across its hull, the dust coming off of its treads, the two-story home that it was about to plow into.

The home was an American home. The story this photograph told was an American story—about urban renewal, industrial decay, brute force, and bullying. But the machine was not a metaphor. In some other city—Detroit, or Baltimore, or even New York—you might have looked at a blasted-out neighborhood and thought, "It's as if they'd driven a tank through it." In Oakland, they had used an actual tank.

If you've spent any time in Oakland, there's a good chance you've heard of the East Bay Rats Motorcycle Club, which has its clubhouse near the corner of Thirtieth Street and San Pablo Avenue in West Oakland.

The EBRMC is not an especially old club; the Rats formed with just a few members in 1994. But they made a quick impression, getting into barroom brawls and backroom gangbangs, and leaving tread marks—the gummy residue of burnouts, spinouts, and other cool motorcycle moves—up and down the length of San Pablo Avenue. The Rats installed a boxing ring behind their clubhouse, and hosted fight parties that drew thousands of people. They became known for their Fourth of July fireworks displays, which eclipsed Oakland's own, and for shooting guns, smashing cars, setting motor scooters on fire, and blowing propane tanks up in public. The Rats burned sofas, old pianos—whatever they could get their hands on—out on the San Pablo median strip. Once, they'd dragged a full-size fighter jet engine out into the avenue, angled it upward, and used it to incinerate the neighborhood lampposts. And in 2001, the Rats did something that the Bay Area's residents still haven't forgiven them for. That summer, a gray whale beached itself on the San Francisco shoreline. "It had the shape of whale, flukes, rising backbone, long, tapering head and bird-beak upper jaw resting on the wider yoke of the lower jaw," the journal of the California Academy of Sciences had reported. "During the night, someone had climbed on top of it and painted in large yellow letters, 'East Bay Rats Motorcycle Club.'"

The Rats went on to tag more whales. They added more members and continued to attract attention. In 2005, the audience of a cable show called *Only in America* watched the show's host, a Pulitzer Prize–winning journalist named Charlie LeDuff, fight a three-hundred-pound Rat named Big Mike, and lose. Four years later, Gavin McInnes fought Meathead Eric in back of the clubhouse. Eric was a mixed martial artist. McInnes, a cofounder of *Vice* magazine, was filming the pilot for a reality show called *The Immersionist*. Eric beat him senseless in less time than it would have taken them to have watched a TV commercial, and *The Immersionist* was not picked up for distribution.

The Rats were hard to pin down, gather up, or control for any length of time. They wore black leather, broke people's bones. They had mixed feelings about the cameras. And they'd formed in response to conditions—economic collapse, real devastation wrought by the crack epidemic—that did not fold themselves neatly into the narrative arcs of half-hour reality shows. In some strange way, the Rats were like Allen's tank, personified and projected fifty years into the future: they did not belong on the city streets. The club would have been a natural starting point for anyone who wanted a deeper understanding of the place that tolerated, even celebrated its presence. But my interest in the EBRMC was more personal—and my interest in the club's president, Trevor Latham, was more personal still.

CHAPTER TWO

I first met Trevor in the fourth grade, at an elementary school in Huntington Station, Long Island. I was eight, Trevor was a year older, but I still remember the way his house looked, in that first year of Ronald Reagan's first administration: with its two unkempt stories and lawn full of weeds, it looked almost exactly like my house.

Like me, Trevor lived alone with his dad. Like my dad, Trevor's was an aeronautics engineer in one of the nearby military-industrial mills. Our dads had both been athletes, once. In their youth, both of them had raced motorcycles. Now time had caught up with them, twisted a knife. Trevor and I felt the weight of their burdens at home and pushed our own weight around in the school yard. We were nowhere near puberty. But well into adulthood, my memories of Trevor involved punching and kicking, biting, blind fear, and sheer, animal rage.

Why did Trevor pick on me? Because I was the new kid in school—a perpetual new kid, I'd moved several times already.

Or, it was because I was young for my grade and small for my age, bookish, and sad. My parents had split up a few years before then, and I'd gone to live with my mother in Pittsburgh. Then my mother died and I went to live with my father, near Boston. Then my dad lost one job, and then another, and we moved again, and again, tumbling through the American dream before ending up out on Long Island. I know now that Trevor had had his own sorrows. But back then, I was too young to register them. To me, Trevor was simply a bully: someone who would wait for me, out by the schoolhouse door every morning, and threaten me with the things he would do to me once school got out. The threats were not idle: I'd come home bruised, sometimes covered in dog shit, and if the next day was a school day, I'd wake up expecting more of the same. By the end of fourth grade, I'd begun to play hooky. By the end of fifth grade, I was flunking my classes. At the end of sixth grade, my dad and I moved yet again—a move that was followed by still other moves, until, five years later, I dropped out of high school and moved, one last time, to New York. By then my bully had turned into a shadow, and then just a name, which I'd remembered because "Trevor Latham" was such a good name for a bully. The truth is that, by our late teens, neither one of us would have recognized the other.

Decades passed. Then, one day in 2006, I came across Trevor's alumni note (Walt Whitman High School, Class of 1990): "I moved to California, became a bouncer, and started a motorcycle club," it read. To me, this made sense: my grade-school nemesis had become a professional bully. Nevertheless, it was startling.

Trevor's club had a website—a no-frills affair with a splash page that read:

6

Clicking through, I saw scans of old fight-party flyers, advertisements for pole-dancing contests, and photographs of wild pigs, or boars, that the Rats had hunted and gutted and laid in a line. Below them, there was a photo of a man who'd posed with his back to the camera. A massive tattoo of the East Bay Rats' logo, a stylized rat skull, took up the whole of his back. The caption read, "Trevor and his new Tattoo." But I couldn't see Trevor's face in the photo, and there wasn't that much more to go on. The Rats hosted bands at the clubhouse and charged ten dollars for boxing lessons. They sold swag—support stickers, and sweatshirts that read:

EAST BAY FIGHT NIGHT
Support Consensual Bloodshed

The website's "buy" link still worked, but others went nowhere or led to pages that said, "Coming Soon." But there, on the home page, I saw one more photo, of two men fighting in front of a crowd. The first man was throwing a punch—a right cross. The second man had thrown his hands up, defensively. He had dark, curly hair, a face streaked with blood, an alarmed expression. He looked, a little, like me. But it was the first man I couldn't stop looking at. He was light-skinned and shirtless, in black jeans and boxing gloves, and he was squinting, which made it harder to make out his features. Still, the punch he was throwing was one I remembered from childhood.

Could this man have been Trevor?

I got up and went to the kitchen, where I drank one beer, and then another, and smoked the first cigarette I'd had in months. Back at my desk, I enlarged the photo, again and again, until I was staring at pixels.

I thought it was Trevor.

I couldn't be sure.

But I felt an old shudder and knew then that I would call him, write him, or, perhaps, write about him.

That week, Trevor was all that I talked about. "You'll have to go out there and fight him," friends said, and I got the sense they were only half-joking. But I wore glasses, wrote book reviews then, and worked as an adjunct professor. Trevor was a biker, a bouncer, a boxing instructor. He taught where the organs were, how to hurt people.

"I've fought him already," I said.

I did not want to fight him again. But I did want the story to tell. His story, mine—whatever it was that had tied us together, back then, and carried us into the now. One night, I worked up a pitch, which I sent to a friend of a friend who worked at *Gentleman's Quarterly*. Then I dialed the number on Trevor's website.

It turned out to be Trevor's number.

He was out at a bar when I reached him. A grumble of voices crowded the line and I had a moment to wonder: would Trevor remember me now? For all I knew, he was brain-damaged, crazy—all of the fights that he'd been in, the blows to the head. I didn't know quite what to picture or say.

"Hello?" said Trevor.

"We knew each other in grade school," I said.

There was a pause. Then I heard my own name.

"Alex?"

"Trevor?"

"I was just talking about you," he said. "Yesterday, telling a friend all about you. My friend told me, 'One day, you'll walk down some dark alley. At the end, you'll meet Alex Abramovich.'"

I was taken aback. Trevor didn't sound damaged, or crazy, or even surprised. He spoke slowly, carefully, assigning equal weight to each word.

"My friends all say I should fight you," I told him.

"What do you think?"

"That they're being ridiculous."

Trevor laughed. Then he asked where I was, and I told him that I was at home, in my apartment in Queens. He asked what I did for a living. I told him that, too. Then he took down my number and said that he'd call me back after he'd closed up the bar.

He never did. I tried him again, calling and texting in the days that followed. There was no response. Then I heard from *GQ* and texted again: "I pitched our story to *GQ*," I wrote. "They're interested."

This time he replied right away. "If you want to be Hunter S. Thompson about it," said Trevor, "you can stay at the clubhouse, ride a bike, and live the life for a while."

I told him that I'd book a ticket that night.

CHAPTER THREE

Two weeks later I landed in San Francisco. It was past midnight, on a crisp night in early October. I was worn out from the flight. But Trevor had texted and asked me to meet him at work, so I picked up the rental car *GQ* had paid for and crossed the Bay Bridge into Oakland.

The city's downtown was deserted and spooky, with abandoned buildings and dark parking lots. The traffic lights all blinked yellow. But when I pulled up to the bar I heard music—a muffled roar coming up from the inside. A sandwich board on the sidewalk read: THE RUBY ROOM. Beneath it, someone had written in chalk: COME DROWN YOUR SORROWS IN BEER.

I parked a few feet in back of some motorcycles, put on my jacket, and pulled out my phone. I was texting Trevor when the bar door swung open and five or six bikers spilled out. They wore black leather vests over black leather jackets, with the East Bay Rats' logo—flanked top and bottom by the club's name—sewn on the backs of their vests. The men were enormous, with furrowed brows, slicked-back hair, and tattoos. They were smiling, high-fiving—visibly happy, visibly drunk. They looked like twenty-first-century Vikings, and when I got out of the car they ignored me.

"Trevor?" I said.

One of the Vikings turned toward me, and let a few beats go by before answering.

"Trevor's inside," said the man. "Who are you?"

I told him, and found that he knew me already.

"He's the writer," another Rat said.

"This is the kid Trevor bullied?"

"The way Trevor remembers, this guy bullied him."

I smiled at the thought, and then the Rats smiled, started laughing, and formed a huddle around me. Joking and jostling, they hustled me into the bar.

The Ruby Room's walls were done in red velvet. Red lightbulbs hung from the ceiling and off to our left a long, wooden counter with red padding around its edges stretched, several yards, toward the back of the bar. To our right there was a wooden partition, into which the image of a blindfolded woman had been carved. The Ruby Room had once been a courthouse bar for lawyers and prosecutors who worked around the corner at the Alameda County courthouse. Lady Justice, in her blindfold, was all that was left of that history now. But there was a bar stool behind the partition, and a vitrine above it with photos and newspaper articles, some of which dated back to the middle of the previous century. The most recent clip, from the *East Bay Express*, was an award citation that read: BEST OF THE EAST BAY, 2006.

BEST MOTORCYCLE CLUB
East Bay Rats
Most wrathful things
on two wheels

The bar was packed with punk rockers, women in baby-doll dresses, bikers, and tough guys who might have been boxers or thugs. Some off-duty cops were set up in a booth by the door—the Rats introduced me—and the cops, who were friendly enough, bought a round, then two rounds, then three. As I drank them, I almost forgot about Trevor. At some point, a scuffle broke out in the back of the bar. The Rats kept on joking and jostling each other. The cops didn't even look up. But way in the back the crowd parted and there, in the center, I saw him.

Trevor was dressed, like the rest of the Rats, in black leather. Like the other Rats, he was enormous—almost twice the size of the man he was holding, with a clenched fist, up against the bar's back wall. He had closely cropped hair, a goatee, almond-shaped eyes, and an aquiline nose. There was nothing familiar about him, I thought. And yet, I knew him immediately.

I watched as the smaller man put his head down. Trevor let go and the crowd closed around them. I got up and excused my way back to the end of the bar, but when I got there, both men were gone. In front of me, there was a DJ booth. To my left was a passage that led to the bar's back room, which was dark and smoky, with wood paneling, banquettes, and a pool table. I walked in, and through the smoke I saw him again. Trevor was sitting alone on one of the banquettes, lit by the glow of his cell phone. When he put the phone down, I felt mine buzz.

"Here?" Trevor had texted.

I walked over to him and said, "Here."

Trevor smiled when he saw me, stood up, and bent down to give me a hug. His jacket gave off a faint animal smell. The top of my head came up, just about, to his collar.

"I didn't know if you'd made it," he said.

We sat at the bar, drinking, not saying too much, staring back at ourselves in the mirror. The cops had gone home, followed by the Rats and the rest of the Ruby Room's customers. At some point, the music shut off and a bartender came out and sat down beside us.

"Ride home?" she asked, as she counted the evening's receipts.

"Yep," Trevor said.

It was the first thing he'd said in a while.

In the days leading up to my flight out to Oakland, Trevor and I had fallen into a rhythm—e-mailing, mostly at night, after Trevor had closed the bar and I'd finished grading papers.

Early on, he had written: "I remember waiting for our dads to pick us up, because we'd been fighting again. Neither of them would be angry. Just disappointed. That was so much worse, compared to their anger."

"I remember waiting for you," I replied. "The feeling you'd get when you knew you were going to end up in a fight—I can remember how scary that was. But my father would tell me that, if I backed down, things would only get worse."

I could still hear the man's voice: "Fight!" he would say, and so I would fight—to defend myself, to assert myself, and sometimes (just sometimes) to stick up for kids who were even smaller and weaker than I was. And I'd found out that my dad had been right: if I fought enough, it would stop all the fighting—in that school, at least. The violence had had its own vicious logic. But the fear was something I'd never quite copped to until it came up in my conversations with Trevor.

Trevor wrote: "Waiting was the hardest part. But as far as I remember you and me, I think it was the typical grade-school fight story. Two guys fight then become best friends. But the funny thing with us is we never admitted to being friends. We were always archenemies, plotting deeply to hurt one another at some point. I don't remember us ever having one knockdown fight outside of school or on the playground. We were both far too emotional for that. What I remember is fighting in class. So we would always get broken up and I don't think there was ever a winner or loser per se. I think we became friends because we'd be stuck waiting for the vice principal and made to do punishments together, like cleaning erasers."

"Friends who won't admit it sounds right," I replied, but that wasn't really the case. I didn't remember a friendship with Trevor. When he said that we used to play chess, I couldn't remember that, either.

"The only time I actually feel bad and will apologize for," Trevor told me, "is one time I was trying to kick you and you were trying to get away and in doing so almost knocked over a bookcase. The teacher caught you and not me and you said, 'It wasn't my fault—it was *him*.' I didn't say shit. I didn't fess up. I'm not sorry that I was kicking you. I'm sorry I didn't fess up."

I didn't remember *any* of this, while Trevor recalled so much more, and in such detail, that I became jealous of how clear his memories were. Then I began to think about other bullies, at other schools I had gone to. There had been several that I had all but forgotten, and it struck me now, for the first time, that I might have conflated them, over the years, blamed all their actions on Trevor—simply because I'd remembered his name. Could I have been that unfair? And, if I had been, I wondered, how much more would there be to remember?

"Do you think that you were a bully?" I'd asked him.

There was no reply. But on the day of my flight Trevor wrote me again.

"You can tell your friends that I don't want to fight you either," he said.

* * *

14

Trevor had called me a cab from the bar, and on the morning after our meeting I took BART back down to downtown Oakland and walked a few blocks to the Ruby Room. My rental car was still parked there, a few feet away from the door. There was a library across the street—it took up the whole block and had a half-dozen people camped out in front of it, passed out in sleeping bags, small tents, and boxes. At the end of the block was a lake, which I walked to as I waited for Trevor. The buildings around it were grand: the WPA-era courthouse, made out of granite and exposed concrete; a long Beaux Arts building with gigantic arches, monumental bas-relief sculptures, and an inscription that ran the length of the building and read: AUDITORIUM OF THE CITY OF OAKLAND DEDICATED BY THE CITIZENS TO THE INTELLECTUAL AND INDUSTRIAL PROGRESS OF THE PEOPLE. But the lake itself was polluted, reeking, and covered with algae, and the auditorium had been fenced off. I walked down to the water, pulling my T-shirt up over my nose: the smell (rotten eggs) was too much to take in. Then I heard the roar of a motorcycle, turned, and saw Trevor pull up to the bar on his Rat bike—a mean-looking sports bike that Trevor had painted a flat, industrial black.

He was carrying a spare leather jacket, which he held up and waved, and a spare helmet, which he tossed to me as I approached. Inside the bar, he pulled out an electric kettle and made us two cups of tea. Then we sat down to wait for J.J., the Rat who would be meeting us there.

I was still sleepy, hungover, but also excited and nervous—that morning, I would be riding a motorcycle. Trevor said that, for my first ride, I would need a bike that was smaller and lighter than his. Trevor's motorcycle was fickle and powerful; it had the same weight-to-power ratio as a Formula One racing car, he told me. But, along with his Rat bike, Trevor's friend J.J. owned a dirt bike—a 650cc Kawasaki.

"It's not a starter bike," Trevor said. "But it's not the hardest thing to learn on."

I said, "Whatever you think works for me."

"Did you meet J.J. last night?" Trevor asked.

I told him that J.J. had been the first Rat I'd met—the one I'd mistaken for Trevor—and the one I'd talked to the most once we'd gone into the bar.

J.J. had been friendly enough, but intense, with a white wifebeater on beneath his black leather jacket and a leopard-print wrap on his head. J.J. had been a bodybuilder, a college fullback, a Golden Gloves boxer, and a soldier, and he had maintained the physique that had gotten him through five deployments—two of them in combat, once in Kosovo and then at Abu Ghraib. His Rat bike had a machete strapped to its side—"It's not concealed, so it's not illegal," J.J. had said—and a license plate that he could flip up or down, accordingly, in the presence of anyone who took a special interest in the number. Sometimes, he'd said, the Rats would "light it up"—play cat and mouse—with the local police. Essentially, J.J. told me, there was no way that the cops could catch up to, much less outrun, a Rat bike.

Now, he pulled up on the Kawasaki—a bike that was much taller than I'd expected it to be—and parked on the sidewalk in front of the bar.

"Where we going?" he asked as he flipped up his visor.

"Track's the best place to learn," said Trevor. And so, we went to the track, with Trevor and me in the rental and J.J. roaring after us on his dirt bike, weaving through traffic, pulling wheelies whenever he got a clear stretch. Other drivers gave him a wide berth. I couldn't keep my eyes off him.

"Is J.J. showing off, or does he always ride like that?"

"Yep," Trevor said.

We retraced the walk I had taken that morning, heading west, past the BART station and city hall, before turning north onto San Pablo Avenue. Here, there were welfare hotels, empty lots, liquor stores. Corner boys eyed us from their corners. Out in the avenue, people pushed shopping carts full of cans and bottles, blocking the traffic, ignoring drivers who yelled and honked at them.

This was Trevor's stretch of West Oakland.

"There," he said, pointing across the avenue.

I saw a body shop and an abandoned building. Sandwiched between them there was a squat, one-story structure with blacked-out windows and a large black sign with block letters that read: EAST BAY RATS MOTORCYCLE CLUB.

"Clubhouse?" I asked.

"Yep," said Trevor.

"Should we stop?"

"Nope."

A few minutes later, we crossed the border to Berkeley, with J.J. still riding, maniacally, on one wheel behind us. A municipal street sign read: NUCLEAR FREE ZONE. Then we turned left, toward the water, and arrived at Golden Gate Fields.

It happened to be a horse-racing track. For a moment, I was disappointed; I had been expecting a track for motorcycles. But, it turned out, we had come for the parking lot, which was enormous and empty. For our purposes, it would be perfect.

I gave Trevor the keys to the rental car and watched as J.J. pulled up beside us, got off the bike without turning it off, removed his helmet, and dropped his pants. He was wearing bikini briefs and had shin guards strapped around his legs. He took the shin guards off, tossed them over to me, and I put them on over my jeans. Then I zipped up the jacket that Trevor had brought—it was heavy and armored, a real racing jacket—put on Trevor's helmet, and lifted the visor.

"Ready," I said.

Slight at it was, compared to a full-size motorcycle, the

Kawasaki was high off the ground. It came way up above my waistline and was surprisingly heavy. The only way that I could touch the ground, once I had gotten on it, was to lean the bike all the way over, and when I did this, it took all of my strength just to keep from dropping the bike.

"Ready?" Trevor asked.

I did not know a thing about motorcycles. But I did know a bit about motorcycle crashes. There were doctors in my family. I could still feel the imprint of a very old crash on the back of my father's seventy-one-year-old skull. I might have asked J.J.: Where is the clutch? How much gas should I give it? How will I stop? But the helmet had cut the bike's roar down to a rumble, and the armored jacket felt like something that a knight might have worn into battle. Instead of speaking, I pictured cavalry charges, tasted the blood on my tongue. It was exhilarating, and idiotic.

"Ready," I said.

Trevor and J.J. moved back from the bike. I lowered the visor, pulled back on the throttle, and readied myself. But what happened next happened too quickly for me to take in. For a moment I seemed to be flying, with my hands stretched out in front of me. Then I was lying—flat on my stomach—down on the concrete.

The bike was four or five yards in back of me. Pushing up on my elbows, I turned my head and saw J.J., who had a piece of chalk in his hand and was tracing a line around the motorcycle. When he was done tracing, J.J. took a bottle of lighter fluid out of his jacket and squirted the length of the line. Then he took out a match and set the chalk line on fire.

"It's a ritual," he said as the smoke rose.

"You killed your first bike," said Trevor.

The Kawasaki didn't look damaged. The fire burned out right away. But as he picked up the bike, Trevor told me I'd looped it—wheelied, accidentally, and ridden on the back wheel for just a few yards before losing my grip, letting go of the bike, flying over the handlebars, gliding for fifteen feet or so, falling, and breaking the fall with my hands and my head. This made sense, though nothing was hurting too badly. The armor really had worked, and when Trevor asked if I wanted to try it again, I said, "Sure."

I'd scraped the knuckles on my right hand raw. But it wasn't until I'd climbed back on the bike, and tried once more to grip the throttle, that I realized my left hand was damaged as well. There was no pain or swelling—no feeling at all. But when I tried to close my thumb, the thumb wouldn't respond. Back in New York, doctors at Beth Israel would tell me I'd broken it in a few places; that it would take hours of surgery, months of physical therapy, and tens of thousands of dollars to put all the parts back together.

"To be honest," the surgeon would tell me, "you'll never not feel it again."

For me, at least, fighting was out of the question. I was hors de combat, disabled, benched. But on the night after my accident, the Rats held a Sadie Hawkins dance out at the clubhouse.

As I understood it, a Sadie Hawkins dance was a dance to which women invited the men. As the Rats understood it, the dance would involve women in various states of undress, taking turns at the poles that Trevor had installed on the clubhouse bar, while men in the crowd stuffed dollar bills in their underpants.

There would be fights, Trevor said, though none of the Rats would be fighting. "Tonight," he said, "we're all going to be acting like gentlemen." *GQ* was sending a photographer out, and most of the Rats had decided on formal or semiformal attire. Trevor had put on a tuxedo himself, a rented one with a pre-tied bow tie, and was limping slightly and holding a cane. I was surprised. I hadn't noticed him limping before.

"The pain comes and goes," Trevor told me.

I asked him to tell me the story.

Six years had gone by, but the crash he'd been in had been serious—a blind turn, a drunk driver. Trevor had also been drunk. He'd had a girl on the back of his bike; she had split her head open, and in the hospital doctors told Trevor that he was lucky—the wreck should have killed him—but it wasn't certain he'd ever be able to walk. And yet, the girl had survived, and over the course of several months, Trevor did teach himself to walk again. It was a miracle, the doctors said, and Trevor had taken this as a good sign. After leaving the hospital he'd gone out and gotten a handicapped plate for his Rat bike.

There wasn't that much to do at the clubhouse. I'd arrived early, to help prepare, but a few prospects—would-be Rats, who'd apprenticed to the club in the hopes of becoming full members—had already set up for the party. I ended up asking Trevor to show me around.

The clubhouse contained four rooms. The one Trevor lived in was like a windowless cell, with walls made of plywood, a naked mattress, piles of magazines that covered the floor, and several knives that were scattered about, along with various firearms—handguns and rifles. There was no lock on the door, but, Trevor said, all of his guests would know not to enter. Two of the other rooms were bathrooms, both filthy and, despite a sign that read: IF YOU TAG IN HERE WE WILL LITERALLY, ANALLY RAPE YOU, covered in crud and graffiti. The main room was open and more or less empty, with a concrete floor and folding chairs that were stacked in a corner. Against one wall, there was a boxing dummy. Across its chest the Rats had written: I FUCKED YOUR MOMMA.

The walls themselves were covered in photos, of the Rats

holding guns, riding track bikes, and fighting. One was the fight photo I'd seen on the Rats' website.

"That you?" I asked Trevor. "The shirtless guy?"

"That's J.J.," said Trevor.

Looking closer, I saw that it was, and asked about J.J.'s opponent—the man with the blood on his face.

"That's Franco," said Trevor.

"Franco?"

"He's a Rat. He was in the Navy, attached to the Marines."

"It's a good photo," I said. "I see the fear in his face."

"Have you seen *Black Hawk Down*?" Trevor said. "Franco was there, in Mogadishu. He got shot—in the chest—and flatlined, right there in the field. Franco's buddies brought him back to life; he stayed conscious for however long it took him to give them instructions. So, I don't think that that's fear that you're seeing."

"You don't think that's his blood on his face?"

"It's his blood," Trevor said. "But the fear's something you're bringing into it."

I took this in, and outside, I could see, the Rats had begun to arrive at the party.

They pulled up by themselves, or with dates on the backs of their Rat bikes, which they parked in a neat line in front of the clubhouse. Like Trevor's bike, theirs were Japanese sports bikes. They had dented gas tanks, scrapes, gouges, gunpowder burns, and looked like they'd been crashed, multiple times, and put back together with duct tape and twist ties. All of them had been painted a flat, industrial black—an aesthetic that brought *Mad Max* to mind—though the Rats themselves, in their suits and tuxedos, had cleaned up nicely. As I watched them gather, I pictured them in other cities, holding down office jobs, hiding their tattoos from middle management, fronting punk rock bands at night. For their part, the Rats ignored me entirely. *GQ*'s photographer had flown in that day, and he had their undivided attention.

GQ had wanted to send a combat photographer. But the combat photographers were all out covering actual wars, and the editors had sent the next best thing they could think of—a Dublin-born Irishman, dressed all in denim, who looked like he'd be right at home with the Rats' rough-and-tumble—although, with him, the Rats were all acting like pussycats, joking and jostling in front of the camera. Only Big Mike, the Rat who had beaten up Charlie LeDuff, the journalist, hung back. He was to be the night's referee and was getting into the headspace.

The Rats had not gotten their boxing ring yet. There were no ropes to separate the spectators from the fighters: just two ratty couches, a back fence made out of corrugated metal, and the exterior wall of the building next door. At some point, the yard must have been covered with gravel. Now most of the gravel was gone and two pairs of boxing gloves lay in the dirt. "Those are old gloves," said Big Mike. "The padding's all shot. We've used them for hundreds of fights."

For the Rats, fighting was never a formalized thing. Sometimes they wore gloves and followed Queensberry rules: no wrestling or hugging; no punching below the belt. Sometimes they fought bare knuckled and ignored the rules altogether. Sometimes they fought five on five, "drunks versus stoners," in which case the drunks always carried the day. But now that more strangers were showing up at the Rats' fight nights, the Rats themselves fought less and less.

On the night of the Sadie Hawkins dance, eight men and two women filled out the fight card. The youngest was sixteen, or just a bit older—he had a black eye already and disqualified himself, in the first round, by throwing an elbow at his opponent's head. Then came the punks—skinny guys with Mohawks and Misfits tattoos, and bits of metal studding their faces. They fought viciously and, because they hadn't thought to remove the metal in their faces, bloodily. The photographer was standing with Trevor and me, facing the fighters, our backs to the wall of the building next door. By the end of the third fight, the three of us were flecked with fluids. During the fourth fight, Trevor leaned over and said, "That could have been us, twenty years ago."

I'd never seen so much blood. But Trevor was grinning, slightly. The photographer was grinning, too, and when he showed me a photo he'd taken of Trevor and me, I was surprised to see myself grinning as well. Despite the blood, the fights had all ended quickly. Most of the boxers were smokers. They grew winded, exhausted themselves, collapsed after a few rounds, or crawled off to vomit. The crowd hooted and hollered. A dog ran around, lapping up all the vomit.

As a rule, Trevor said, the girl fights lasted longer.

With the Rats, violence was systemic and systematized from the get-go. To join the club, you had to prospect for a year, working bar duty and cleaning scum off the clubhouse walls. Prospects organized rides that the rest of the Rats were expected to go on. They were expected to fight, at least twice—it didn't matter if they won or lost. Then the club took a vote, and if it was unanimous the prospects were patched in and jumped in—worked over—by all of the Rats, simultaneously. Big Mike had weighed 320 pounds at the time of his beat-down; he'd managed to stay on his feet for a full fifteen minutes. But, in the end, even he had gone down. "There's blood," Trevor said. "Sometimes broken bones. But when else are your friends going to pay so much attention to you?"

"You get to know a man by riding with him, fighting with him, hanging out," J.J. told me. "We prospect you for a while. We don't haze you. We get to know you. And if you've got the strength of character, it's not about how tough you are. It's about how you act when you lose. I've lost fights. We all have. But the Rats, well, we'll break you down. We'll break you down and take a look at you from where *you* are. By the time we're done with you, you got nothing left to prove."

Many Rats came from broken homes, or abusive ones. Several had spent nights or weekends in jail, a few had been to prison, and many more were veterans: Franco, the Rat who'd been shot in Somalia. Davey Fuller, who'd been a marine at Camp David. J.T., the Rats' treasurer, had also been a marine, and J.J. had his five deployments behind him. "Look at me," J.J. had told me. "I'm pretty fucking tough. But I ain't the toughest guy in Oakland. I ain't even the toughest guy on this block. There's a lot of crime here, a lot of folks doing serious dirt. We don't do no dirt. We're together because we're sitting here together in the lower bottom of society. The neighborhood I live in is *called* the Lower Bottoms.

"A lot of us guys have regular, working-class jobs. I'm an electrician. My roommate's a contractor. My other roommate's a tin knocker. One's a machinist, you know? And we gotta keep our bikes running, and our asses from getting fucked up in the streets. Sometimes, when you need backup, a cell phone comes in pretty fucking handy: 'Listen, I need thirty guys right here, right now. A show of force.'

"Ask for thirty, you might get ten. But get ten who are willing to die for you? You can do a lot with that."

All but one of the East Bay Rats' thirty-five members owned guns; the club's rules specified that all of the Rats who could own guns, legally, had to own guns, and Trevor kept a Glock 23, two .45s, three bolt-action Remingtons, two shotguns, and a semiautomatic M1 rifle at the clubhouse. All of the Rats carried knives. But, aside from their disdain for traffic laws and fire ordinances—and with the exception of J.J., who self-identified as a 1%, outlaw biker—the Rats were not outlaws or out-and-out *Sons of Anarchy*–style criminals. They avoided hard drugs. And unlike other, older MCs, the Rats were not racially exclusive. Big Mike was black. Franco was Mexican American. A Rat named Ted spoke pidgin Yiddish and had a borscht-belt comedian's shtick that he dipped in and out of whenever occasions presented themselves. This was startling, because Ted was an improbably large, rough-looking man. It turned out that his father had been a rabbi ("a junkie rabbi," Ted said) from the Bronx.

The club's members cut across other boundaries, as well. A lot of the Rats were working-class guys, or blue-collar guys like Pixar Terry—a prospect who really did work at Pixar, and drove a black late-model Audi—who'd pulled themselves into the white-collar world of IT work. But Big Mike's father was an optometrist, one of the Rats was the son of Art Thoms—who'd played defensive tackle for the Oakland Raiders—and another Rat had married Bruce Nauman, the artist's, daughter. The Rats' fight parties drew lawyers and doctors, and Trevor told me that, once a year, first-year interns from Highland Hospital got drunk and fought at the clubhouse.

"We used to haze them," he said. "But at this point, they just haze each other."

Some Rats had moved up to the hills or out to the suburbs; you didn't see too much of them anymore. But even the Rats who spent most of their time at the bar or the clubhouse had the notion that someone like me had a lot in common with them. "You're like us," they would say, and I would feel flattered, and almost believe them. At first, I thought, they were flattering themselves: saying that they, too, were as civilized, well read, and refined as they imagined me, a writer for *Gentleman's Quarterly*, to be.* But the Rats also meant to suggest that, under our civilized masks, we were all savages—that I was as savage as they were—and that all human beings were basically savages, in ways that Rats and writers were both well equipped to appreciate.

For the most part I liked them and found them easy to get along with. But, as I spent more time with them, I also found that the Rats' conversations could take sudden turns toward the freakish, or flat-out insane. With the Rats, a certain lack of self-consciousness, regarding violence, could be as disturbing as the violence itself.

Outside of the Ruby Room, I ask Big Mike to tell me about his hand—the right one, which, I have noticed, is missing its littlest finger.

Big Mike has dreads and a gentle way about him. He wears glasses and talks in a low, honey drip. "I've never spoken about it before," he tells me. "It's something that's really personal between me and one other person. I tell the world it was an accident. And I tell my brothers it's just 'cause. But really, I made the biggest mistake of my life. And there was no other way for me to show the respect I needed to show, say I'm sorry in a way, and prove my respect and my understanding of how badly I messed up than to offer up that part of myself."

---

*"We're gentlemen, too," Davey Fuller told me, and recited a line from Thorstein Veblen's *Theory of the Leisure Class* to prove his point: "At either end of the social spectrum," he said, "you'll find the gentleman of leisure." When I looked in the book, I couldn't locate the line, but did run across the following: "It is only the high-bred gentleman and the rowdy that normally resort to blows as the universal solvent of differences of opinion."

Mike pulls out a SoBe bottle, takes a swig, and hands it to me—cheap whiskey.

"Have you seen the movie *Bound*? You know that scene where the heavy's all, 'I've only got one question, I'm going to ask you ten times'? And you know he's got a pair of pruning shears? That doesn't work. That shit does not work *at all*. I got a pair of those. A pair of brand-new Felcos. Felco is the best pruning shear you can get. Razor sharp. Really, *really* nice pruners. I get a pair of those, line it up perfectly with the joint, make the slice, and I'm pushing, I'm pushing as hard as I can, and I can't get through the bone. I'm twisting it and I'm twisting it and I can't get the groove. I can't get the fucking thing off. So I stop with that. I'd cut through all the tendons, all the ligaments, and it's kind of hanging there and—use discretion if you can but—it's just there and I'm like, 'Fuck! It's useless now. Gotta get the thing off.' I don't feel like driving to my house for the fucking cleaver. So I go to my buddy's house, borrow a cleaver, and wop the thing off. I had to hit it twice. I'm a lefty, so I did it with my strong hand. I was *dead* sober. It's important to be dead sober for something like that. It's respect. The point is to know what you're doing and why. Because it's important."

I don't know what to say.

Finally I ask him, "Did you present it?"

"Yeah. But it wasn't a formalized thing."

I end up saying, "I'm sorry."

"I'm in my bedroom . . ."

Davey Fuller's drinking coffee, waiting for Trevor to roll out of bed, and this is my second time hearing his story—which he's agreed to repeat, from the start, for the benefit of my tape recorder and the readers of *GQ* magazine.

"I'm drunk," Davey says. "And I'm watching *Breakfast at Tiffany's*. I've got my combat boots on, a pair of PT shorts, my

SS storm trooper's helmet. I'm sitting there drinking a fifth of whiskey because I just broke up with my girlfriend."

I check to make sure the recorder's recording—compared to Big Mike's, Davey's story sounds more or less sane, but I don't want to miss the next part.

"My friends come over. They bring this girl, and the second they come in I can just tell that she needs to get fucked. She's got that nervous, twitchy thing going on, you know? So I tell my friends, 'This girl needs to get fucked!' They sit down, and she's squirming around. She starts poking me. And I'm like, 'Look, baby, the next time you poke me I'm going to fucking choke you.'

"She pokes me again and I just grab her by the throat and pin her down on the bed and say, 'I told you I was going to fucking choke you!'

"She just starts making out with me. So I'm making out with her, then I start fucking her, then my friends get up and leave the room. I'm fucking this girl. We've never met before. And the phone rings. It's my ex-girlfriend, screaming at me that I'm a fucking whore, that she wishes that I was dead. . . . I'm so drunk, I reach under the pillow and grab my .45. I'm like, 'You fucking whore, you wish I was dead? I'll fucking kill myself right now.' And I've got the gun to my head, the phone to the other side of my head, I'm on my elbows, inside this girl who's underneath me, and the girl starts to whimper a bit, so I take the gun and point it to the side of *her* head. To shut her up. Then I get really mad and slam the phone down on the ground. It breaks, I look down, and the girl's quivering and shaking. I'm still inside of her. And I'm like, 'Oh God, I almost blew this girl's brains out!' But I keep fucking her—I point the gun away from her head—and she gets off! I'm like, 'That girl's fucking crazy.' And then, a month later, she calls me up and says, 'Hey, do you want to hang out?'"

Davey sits back and smiles as I put on my headphones to check the recording.

"Did you get it?" he asks.

"I think so," I tell him.

Trevor's own tastes were a bit more vanilla: he was a serial monogamist, with a soft spot for Asian women. But the case could be made that, as the head of a fight club, Trevor was, de facto, a sadist. In fact, he had performed as a sadist, in porno films shot at the Power Exchange, an "eighteen-and-up Adult Alternative Lifestyle/Pansexual Nightclub" in San Francisco. The casting, in that case, was perfect: Trevor showed up in his street clothes and collected a small fee for hitting people—which was something he would have done, quite happily, for free.

At the same time, there were perversions the Rats were less eager to advertise. Years later, I found out that not only had the Rats tagged whales that had washed up on the shore in San Francisco; they'd also climbed up on top of the whales and fucked them, with strap-ons, in their blowholes. Where the strap-ons had come from, I never discovered. But, by and large, the Rats were laissez-faire when it came to sexual matters. And, while their sexual encounters with one another seemed to have been limited to simultaneous liaisons with one or more women, the Rats were not homophobic. Gays and lesbians were welcome at East Bay Rat parties, and there was no rule barring them from the club—although, in practice, no openly gay man had ever applied for membership. Keeping GQ's demographic in mind (it was, after all, a men's magazine), I asked them about Robert Bly and the mythopoetic men's movement. The Rats gave me blank stares; they'd never heard of such things. I had more luck asking about Chuck Palahniuk, and about Palahniuk's novel, Fight Club.

"Even the movie is a bad metaphor for gay S&M," Trevor told me. "Our club's got a lot more in common with *Jackass*."

I found it strange that Trevor's objection had less to do with the metaphor than with the metaphor's quality. But, with a few notable exceptions, the Rats were knuckleheads, not idiots. They were fully aware of the impressions they made on other men—and, especially, on women.

"We're the guys their daddies would hate the most," a Rat named Travis told me.

Travis had grown up in a reform school. He was handsome—a dead ringer for Johnny Knoxville, with the same mischievous aura—and had a tattoo that took up his whole throat. POOR IMPULSE CONTROL, it read.

Seeing his appeal to at least a few demographics, I took Travis at his word.

Some Rats I spoke with still slept with several women a week, alone, or in pairs, or in other groupings that did or did not involve other bikers. Like Trevor, others had more conservative tastes, and, in any case, there were rules concerning their conduct with women, or, at least, with each other's wives and girlfriends. The word "respect" came up often in the Rats' conversations. Hooking up with other Rats' girlfriends was grounds for expulsion and with ex-girlfriends, permissions had to precede actions of any sort. Respect was accorded, also, to women who'd come to the clubhouse to fight.

On the night of the Sadie Hawkins dance, the last two fighters were women. One was skinny and blond, dressed in jeans and a tank top. Trevor knew her by sight, having disqualified her from fighting at previous EBRMC events. She was a head butter, he told me. She should not have been fighting again. All the same, the Rats had decided to let her.

"We'll see if she's still got that rage," Trevor said.

The other fighter was heavily made up, with blood-red lips and heavy eyeliner, long hair she'd dyed black, and a retro, fifties-style Bettie Page dress. She'd come to the party in heels and would have to fight barefoot.

The raven-haired woman kept her head down. She fought defensively, waiting for openings, and there was no head butting. But, in the first round, some punches got through. The brunette began to bleed from her nose. Then, she started to gasp. In the second round she continued to bleed and grew even more winded. Big Mike called the fight in the third, and Trevor raised the blond woman's left arm up over her head as the other woman picked her purse up off the ground and opened her compact.

"I'm asthmatic," she said. "But at least the blood matches my lipstick."

The rest of the week was a blur, with nights out at bars and the days spent with Trevor. We'd go to the clubhouse, drink one-dollar beers from the soda machine he'd installed in the clubhouse and painted a flat, industrial black. Sometimes we'd sit silently. Sometimes we'd talk—about books and movies, about the Rats, about the economics of running a motorcycle club. We talked about boxing and mixed martial arts (which had begun to overtake boxing in the public imagination). We talked about women. We talked about his life in Oakland and mine in New York. What we did not talk about were the things that had brought us together: our childhoods, our families, our fights.

We did not talk about these things so pointedly that, on my last evening in Oakland, we started to talk about not talking about them—talking, and talking, until, bit by bit, we began to touch bottom.

Back on Long Island, Trevor's family had lived down the street from Doug and Billy Yule—brothers who were best known as latter-day members of the Velvet Underground.

After the breakup of VU's last, post–Lou Reed incarnation, the brothers had moved out to California. Trevor told me that, when his parents split, his mother had taken the kids and followed the Yules out to Berkeley.

Trevor's first memories of East Bay were idyllic. Then, his parents finalized their divorce. There was a succession of babysitters. But in time, except for occasional stays with their grandmother, Trevor and his two sisters were left to their own devices. Trevor had seen only a few photographs from this period in his life—ones his grandmother had taken so that the kids would know what they had looked like.

Trevor and his sisters were too young to use the stove, but they were expected to make their own meals. They were skinny and were teased about it in school. Trevor was the youngest and smallest; at home, he became a family scapegoat. In class, he'd begun to act out.

When Trevor was five, he misbehaved and was sent to his bedroom. A few hours passed, and then he was gone. His sisters looked everywhere in the house. Then, they looked out his window and saw a perfect imprint of his body, smashed into the bushes two stories below.

When Trevor was in the first grade, another kid pushed him off the monkey bars. Trevor got up and knocked the boy down, sat on him, and—using the boy's ears as handles—pounded his head, repeatedly, into the asphalt.

When he got home, Trevor told his sisters that that was his "signature move."

"I'd been getting in a lot of fights and losing them," he told me. "Getting bullied a bit, and I figured that my dad could help me with that. I asked to move back. And that's probably why I stayed with him, even when things got bad. I was trying to learn to be tough, like a man."

Trevor's dad, Stuart, had had a short fuse. My own dad had had a bad temper—there had been violent scenes in my home—

but Stuart ripped bedroom doors off their hinges, punched holes in the Sheetrock, raged for days on end. "My father did not punch me often," said Trevor. "But, because the threat was always there, it was always horrifying. He was a very angry, irrational man. He wasn't a drunk—but that somehow would have given him an excuse, or the hope of a cure. In some ways, he was always there for me. I do love him. And I learned a lot from him. But that anger, without reason, was impossible to come to grips with. If there are *always* consequences, there's *never* a consequence. So I just did whatever I wanted. And, eventually, I became very comfortable with violence.

"It's funny," he said. "I never talk about this stuff with friends. It's passé, to whine about your childhood. But here I am talking to you, and you'll put it down in your story and tell the whole world."

"It's good," I said.

From the look he gave me, I could tell Trevor thought I had meant something else—that I could relate, or that talking like this was in some way cathartic. But I hadn't meant that at all. What I'd meant was that it was good for our story.

"You've got your intellectual life in New York," Trevor said. "I'm at the top of lowbrow culture in Oakland. But if we wanted to, we could switch places. I could go back to school, and write, and join your society. You could learn to ride a bike, and fight, and join mine."

Despite my fiasco with J.J.'s bike, I thought that this might have been more or less true.

"Writing *is* fighting," I said.

"Who said that?"

"I said it."

"Who said it, really?"

"Muhammad Ali."

"That's really good. But I don't think we fought much more than five or six times. I only remember two. Once, when you almost knocked over the bookcase. The other one was in front of the blackboard. You were swinging at my body, fighting with everything you had. As if you were trying to kill me."

"Trevor," I said. "I probably *was* trying to kill you."

Just then it struck me, again, that Trevor might not have been all that bad, and that, maybe, just maybe, I hadn't been all that blameless—that we really did have more than a few things in common. Perhaps the difference between us wasn't that he'd been a bully and I'd been the victim of his bullying; perhaps it was that I'd done my best to forget all the fights that I'd been in, while Trevor had tried to remember them all. Either way, Trevor was right: I *did* relate. In its broad outlines, my upbringing had not been that different from his. We'd both been wounded in similar ways. Both of us had survived. And Trevor had grown strong enough to rule over a mass of violent and contradictory impulses—which had manifested themselves, in his case, quite obviously, as the members of a motorcycle club.

There was something admirable about it, I thought: he'd become a fighter, I'd become a writer. Both of us had followed our muse. Thinking about this made me feel strong, too, and resilient in ways I had not felt before when I'd thought of my dad and my own, shitty childhood.

But then, on the red-eye back from San Francisco, I had the first of several panic attacks. My hand began to hurt. I felt claustrophobic and started to sweat, and when I closed my eyes I saw Trevor's face, and the faces of other children I'd fought. Some of the faces belonged to kids who'd hit me. Others belonged to the kids I had hit. All of them were faces I'd spent my adult life forgetting.

I couldn't remember the last time that I'd felt so sad.

CHAPTER FOUR

I drifted off in a cab from the airport and woke up to find that the driver had taken a wrong turn on the way back to Astoria. We'd ended up in some odd, affluent corner of Queens. The houses were immense and ostentatious, with actual lawns, three-car garages, and fountains—the works. It was like the neighborhood that Ray Liotta and Lorraine Bracco move to in *Goodfellas*.

We were hopelessly lost.

"*Goodfellas*?" I asked, drowsily.

"De Niro," said the taxi driver. His accent, thick Mancunian, was murder on the vowels.

"*Taxi Driver*—you must have liked that one."

"I like the later ones, too," he said, defensively. No Englishman could have sounded so foreign to someone who'd grown up speaking American English.

"*Ronin*," I said. It was the last halfway decent De Niro flick that I could think of.

"*Meet the Fockers*. Now *that* was a good one."

It occurred to me that in Manchester, *Meet the Fockers* might have had the same impact that Jerry Lewis had had on Parisians in 1965. To a Mancunian, *Focker* sounded exactly like "fucker."

"That *was* a good one," I agreed, and for that the driver helped carry my suitcase upstairs.

My hand was still hurting (it actually throbbed), and I was sweating now, and feeling sick. I put my backpack down, went to the kitchen, and swallowed some pills. When I woke up, a day later, I saw that Trevor had e-mailed me.

"Memory is a funny thing," he had written. "If you tell a story the same way enough times you actually start to remember it that way. Before meeting you again I should have written down everything I remembered. Now my memory is tampered by your presence. But you seem very much the same. Your mannerisms and expressions."

It was a nice note. But I was really in pain now, panicking, slightly, feeling angry, and starting to have evil thoughts—about Trevor, the week I had spent with the Rats, and, especially, the bike that they'd put me on. Why had that bike been so big? Couldn't they have started me out on a real starter bike? Some old Honda? Or, even, a scooter? The more I thought about it, the more upset I became—not only with Trevor and J.J.—but with myself. I'd agreed so quickly to go along with their plan.

Feeling humiliated, I let a day pass, then a week. Then months had passed and I hadn't replied to Trevor's e-mail. That summer, *GQ* published my story. Trevor texted to tell me that the Rats had liked it; that it had gotten a few of them laid. But when publishers e-mailed my agent to see if I'd turn the article into a book, I told them I wasn't interested.

"I think I'm finished with Oakland," I said. And for a long time I was.

* * *

In the years that followed, Astoria changed, became less diverse, more expensive, and my friends moved on. A close friend fell ill—a faulty heart valve—and died on his way to intensive care. Another friend gave up on office jobs, joined the army, and shipped to Afghanistan. Marriage, tenure, or better jobs in cheaper places caused other friends to move away, and at the same time, my own work in New York began to go badly. Several years into a book I'd been writing, I'd stalled and gone into a tailspin. Everything I wrote seemed plain wrong to me. I kept teaching, and wrote shorter pieces. Every so often, something of mine appeared in a paper or magazine. But, without exception, the places I wrote for had all cut back on their budgets. To supplement my income, I took an editing job at an Internet company. On my first day at work, the company's founder gave me a present—a long, impenetrable book by an obscure Russian mystic. At least it wasn't Ayn Rand, I thought. But, a few days later, the founder called me into his office and, after asking what I had thought of the book, tasked me with helping him choose between corporate slogans: "Traverse the Internet" was the first one he'd come up with. "Vainglorious reportage because we care" was the other.

I lasted three months before finding a better editing job, which ended when the next recession hit, causing my boss to announce to shareholders that he was "getting out of content" entirely. And so, in the summer of 2010, I had no work and no friends left in the neighborhood. For the first time in ages I felt like a stranger in Queens. Then, in October, Trevor passed through New York City.

He'd ridden his Rat bike cross-country, taking the northern route—a straight shot up Interstate 80, which runs door-to-door from the Bay to New York, through Nevada, northern Utah, Wyoming, Nebraska, and the upper Midwest. He'd called me from Indiana: would I mind if he stayed on my couch? The next evening, he knocked on my door.

He had not changed—he was lumbering and large—but his hair had begun to turn gray. And, I could see, he was hurting. A Rat bike is not a touring machine, and the road had done real damage to Trevor's skeletal system. His limp had become an exaggerated, Frankensteinian stagger, and following a hug he dropped his bag and lurched straight from the door to my living-room futon. He sat there for a long time before taking off his leather jacket and dropping it onto the rug. He bent over slowly to remove one motorcycle boot, and then another. He looked out of place in my apartment. But, as I opened a beer for him, I hoped that he felt at home.

Trevor said that he was planning to go to his high school reunion, his twentieth, and to see Stuart, his father. When I asked about the Rats, he said they'd slowed down, gone through some drama and a few rough patches. More club members had gotten married; a few had had kids. J.J. had been expelled from the club, and two Rats—Big Nate McMahon and Norton Aaron Fuller—had crashed on their bikes and died.

I remembered Big Nate, who'd been hulking and quiet, and Trevor's old friend since before the Rats had even formed. He had crashed late at night after leaving the Ruby Room. Nate had learned just that morning that his girlfriend was pregnant, freaked out all day long, then gone to another Rat's bachelor party. Afterward, he had gone to the bar and kept on drinking. Trevor was at the bar, too, and after the crash he had rushed to the scene, where paramedics were cutting Nate's clothes off. A cop had pulled him aside and said, "I'm not supposed to be telling you this, but your friend is having a really hard time."

Trevor had been too stunned to understand.

"I was like, 'All right.' It never crossed my mind that the cop knew, and was trying to help me see, that Nate wasn't going to make it."

Norton Aaron's crash had been more mysterious and among the Rats, there were rumors that J.J. was somehow involved.

Given the way that the Rats lived, drank, and rode, it was odd that the club had existed as long as it had with just the two tragedies. But two deaths, in such quick succession, of members who'd been so close to the club's core, coupled with the expulsion of one central member—I couldn't imagine the stress that had caused. I was upset, not only for Trevor, but for all of the Rats I had met. I had many questions, which I formulated as I got up to get us more beer. But when I came back from the kitchen, Trevor was asleep, still sitting upright on the futon.

In the morning, Trevor asked if he could borrow some basic tools: a wrench, some screwdrivers. Stuart's water heater was broken, he said, and he was going out to Long Island to check it. I offered to come along. In a Zipcar, we drove out toward our old town, passing Hempstead, Levittown, and Farmingdale, where my father had worked.

I drove and Trevor texted, managing the Ruby Room (where he still worked) from afar and conducting (I guessed) important East Bay Rats business.

"How do you spell 'which'?" he asked, looking up from his iPhone.

"Which which?"

"Not the one with the hat."

"W-h-i-c-h," I spelled.

"Cool."

We passed industrial parks, Taco Bells, gyms. I saw the Ground Round restaurant my dad and I had eaten at once, thirty years earlier.

"I can't believe that's still there," I said.

"Yep. There's a book about it."

"About the Ground Round?"

"About how to spell 'which.'"

We passed more industrial parks, a new high school I did not recognize.

"It's called *Which Witch Is Which*," Trevor said.

"The book?"

Trevor had gone back to his texting.

"And you read it?"

"Yep."

"And you still don't know how to spell 'which'?"

"Yep."

Trevor was right: there *is* a book called *Which Witch Is Which*, which I looked up, later, online. The book was intended for preschoolers. The quoted review, from the *School Library Journal*, read as follows:

> When identical twins Ella and Emily are invited to a Halloween party, they decide to dress as witches. As the party progresses, readers will have fun deciding "which witch is which" by closely watching the games the boys and girls play, the food they eat ("Cowboy chose strawberry, Ella the same"), and colors they choose. The party comes to a festive finale with the thematic question, "Which witch is which?"

This was perfect, I thought. Trevor's story and mine in a nutshell. At least there was some sort of script.

*　*　*

Trevor's dad was an old man in a flat cap, reading a Tea Party pamphlet at the McDonald's in Walt Whitman Mall.

I had expected a much larger man: Trevor years later and heavier. But Stuart was smaller than I was. He was wearing a checked shirt, blue jeans, and a braided belt, and took his glasses off to hug his son. Neither one of them said very much. Then the three of us drove the Zipcar over to our old school.

Like Walt Whitman Mall (which had turned into Walt Whitman Shops), the school had a new name now: Oakwood Elementary had become Oakwood Primary Center. But the building had not been built out and the grounds looked exactly the same, right down to the slides, swings, and jungle gyms. For us, it was like visiting a museum. We walked the perimeter (school was not in session), and I told Trevor that, when I was writing the *GQ* article, I'd called the school and told our story to a secretary. The school had tossed all its old records, she'd said. Our teachers had all retired or died. The lady couldn't help me at all.

"They tossed our permanent records?" said Trevor.

"So she said," I said, and looked up to see Stuart, wandering off toward the Zipcar, leaving us to listen to the creak of our old swing sets.

Trevor had warned me that Stuart was strange. "A crazy hoarder," he'd said, as we'd driven out from Astoria. But Stuart wasn't *that* strange—toward me, he was perfectly pleasant— and toward Trevor he was tender, if a bit tentative. The rages that Trevor had told me about seemed to have burned themselves off long ago. But as we pulled into his driveway I saw that not all was right with the man.

Stuart still lived in the small brown house I had remembered. The front lawn still had the overgrown look of a neglected backyard. There was no front door, I saw no windows where the living room might have been, and this reinforced the impression that the whole house had been spun around and set backward on its foundation. When we entered, through a side door, I saw that the inside was off-kilter, too. There were piles of paper all over the floor and the counters, and the dishes in Stuart's sink were not dirty so much as disused. It looked like it had been a long time since the room had been used for its original purpose.

In what must have been the home's living room, a bay window faced the backyard. It had been covered with fabric. The side window had been covered, too, and mountains of junk mail were piled on the couch and coffee table. Other piles took up most of the floor space and clear plastic bins, marked with masking tape (POCKET NOTEBOOKS; RC RADIO EQUIP-MENT; COMPONENTS) were stacked up to the ceiling. In front of us, there was an old grandfather clock, an old upright piano, and an old painting of two travelers stopped in the woods.

The Lathams were an ancient clan, with roots in north-ern England and a name derived from the Old Norse word *hlatham*, or "barn dweller"—a variation appeared in the *Domesday Book*, in 1086. In America, the first Latham arrived in 1620, on board the *Mayflower*. An eleven-year-old at the time of his landing, William Latham apprenticed to William Bradford; later on, he employed Myles Standish to mow his lawn. He may or may not have had children. But in 1654, a Robert Latham of Plymouth Bay was tried for the death of his own fourteen-year-old apprentice. "*The body of John Walker was blackish and blew, and the skine broken in divers places from the middle to the haire of his head, viz, all his backe with stripes given him by his master, Robert Latham, as Robert him-selfe did testify,*" the coroner's jury reported, and went on to list several other injuries. By the end of proceedings, Robert Latham's property had all been confiscated and he'd been punished, corporally, with the burning of one of his hands—a harsh sentence in a time when the abuse of servants was no great crime. Then again, even by the day's standards, his seemed to have been a notorious case: "*Wee find the flesh much broken of the knees of John Walker and that he did want sufficient food and clothing and lodging, and that the said John did constantly wett his bed and his cloathes, lying in them, and so suffered by it, his clothes being frozen about him; and that the said John was put forth in the extremity of cold . . . and therefore in respect of crewelty and hard usage he died,*" the coroner's jury concluded.

In 1661, the king of England awarded a branch of the Lathams a land grant to help establish Oyster Ponds, a town on the easternmost tip of Long Island's North Fork. To this day, there is a Latham Farm there, and other Lathams are scattered all over Long Island. (Until recently, Stuart's older brothers ran Latham Brothers, a lumber concern in Northport.) Across America—in Kansas, Ohio, Tennessee, downstate Illinois, and upstate New York—you can still find towns and communities named after a Latham. In Oakland, at the intersection of Broadway and Telegraph—Oakland's main streets, along with San Pablo Avenue—there is a plaza called Latham Square.

The Lathams had done well for themselves: gone on to become lawyers and architects, poets and pastors, composers, journalists, baseball players. They had first names like Milton, Mercy, Eliab, and Absalom, fought in every American war, invented the QWERTY keyboard and one of the first motion picture projectors.* Stuart himself had grown up in baronial

---

*On his mother's side, Trevor believed himself to be descended from Martha Washington and Pocahontas.

splendor, with eight bathrooms, or twelve (he no longer remembered), in a waterfront mansion on Long Island's North Shore. But, while Trevor was still at Oakland Elementary, Stuart had lost his job at McDonnell Douglas. He looked for work, without finding it, and lived off his inheritance. Trevor remembers him spending more and more of his time sitting around the house. Then all the money was gone, and now, back in Stuart's house, I saw that there wasn't enough space for three people to sit. Trevor and I stood by the piano as Stuart went upstairs to rummage around. When he returned, he was holding a rifle.

"That's a beautiful thing," Trevor said.

Stuart sat on the piano bench and placed the rifle across his lap.

"One time I made a mistake," Stuart said. "I saw a woodchuck. It was no farther away than from here to the top of the stairs. I shot it, and it exploded in this big cloud, a red cloud of steam. I was trying to get out of it—not breathe it in. My God, there was nothing left! That was so stupid."

"Oh, yeah," said Trevor. "Lots of woodchucks on the roads out here. I'm amazed—we don't get them in California."

"Oh, yeah?" Stuart said.

Then Trevor mentioned the plumbing. I followed him down to the bowels of the house, where piles of cardboard were stuffed, along with stacks of old wood, toolboxes, paint cans, and rattraps, more plastic bins, suspended implements, clotheslines, propane lanterns, an uncoiled garden hose. Trevor pulled out a small flashlight, the one that he used to check IDs at the bar, and tapped the side of a large water heater.

"Not working?"

"Nope."

"How does he shower?"

"Beats me," Trevor said and called out to Stuart, upstairs. "You got a bucket?"

"It'll take a lot more than a bucket!" his dad hollered back, and though we lingered some more in the basement, we ended up leaving things there as we'd found them.

Trevor and I spent the next few days in Manhattan. He wanted to visit the American Museum of Natural History ("they look like we do when you skin them," Trevor said, as we stood in front of a bear that had been stuffed and raised up on its hind legs), to eat lobster rolls, to see *Jackass 3*, which had just come out in 3-D. We did all of those things, walked around, and made small talk. My girlfriend's parents were in town that week, and I took Trevor to meet them for dinner. He was polite, unobtrusive, an easy houseguest, and Lucy, my girlfriend, could not understand how we could have been enemies. That Friday night, Trevor went to his high school reunion and stayed out at a motel on Long Island. On Saturday, Lucy and I threw a party for a friend of ours. Trevor arrived in the middle of it.

I'd been wondering for days about Norton Aaron, about J.J., and J.J.'s expulsion from the club. But, wanting to be a good host, I was wary of bringing up the world that Trevor was taking a break from, and kept my questions to a minimum. I knew already that Trevor moved at his own pace, which was slow, and that the best way to get answers from him was often to just stick around and wait until something happened. But now, to my surprise, Trevor took the initiative. He talked to everyone in the room. He made a point of it: if he had not talked to you yet, he'd walk over, introduce himself, shake your hand, and ask about you. He was genuinely curious, and he seemed to know at least a little about every subject that came his way. It was a side of him I hadn't seen—a charming one—and I thought, yes, perhaps he could have slipped easily into my world.

I thought about this some more in the days that followed.

And when Trevor left, just before Halloween, I found that I missed him and wished that I'd asked him much more. There was more to know, more to write about, and I was not teaching that year. My schedule was as clear as it had ever been, and Lucy and I had already been talking about California, which her sister and brother were both moving to.

"Why not leave now?" I asked her. "I'll fly out, find us a sublet. We'll stay out there for six months and see."

"Why not?" said Lucy.

We ended up staying for close to four years.

CHAPTER FIVE

Trevor took a slow southern route home, riding his Rat bike through North Carolina, Tennessee, Arkansas, Oklahoma, and the Southwest. He stayed with acquaintances, cousins, and friends and took time off to go hunting. He was still on the road when I landed in Oakland.

I crashed with friends who'd moved out to California a few years before me and spent my time setting up—buying an old car and looking for a place that Lucy and I could move into. My friends had kids, cats, cars, day jobs, a million errands to run. It was as if they were still living on New York City time. But it took me just a few days to adjust to the local schedule. I drove to the seashore at Point Reyes, and up to Bodega Bay, where Hitchcock had shot *The Birds*. I hiked in Muir Woods, and toured Napa and Sonoma, where the California light made the valleys and vineyards look like matte paintings. In the afternoons I read books about Oakland—depressing books with depressing titles like *American Babylon: Race and the Struggle for Postwar Oakland*, *No There There: Race, Class, and Political Community in Oakland, Bump City: Winners and Losers in Oakland*—along with depressing articles about the city, and a depressing case study, from the sixties, called *Oakland's Not for Burning*. In the evenings, I drove around and tried to locate the places I'd read about. I stopped by the Ruby Room several times but didn't recognize anyone there. I drove to the East Bay Rats clubhouse—a new sign on the front door read: SORRY FOR THE DISTURBANCE. But from what I could tell when I knocked, no one was around to make one.

Trevor's stretch of San Pablo looked like the ass end of some Potemkin village, or like a movie set that had been abandoned and taken over by the local bad element. There were street-walkers, corner kids, shopping-cart people, any number of liquor stores. Two Star Market, one block north of the club-house, had lost its liquor license and now sold propane light-ers and bottles of quarter water. A tiny, triangular park across the street had become an open-air drug market. Months later, I learned the park's name: Saint Andrews Plaza. But in all my time in Oakland, I never heard anyone call it anything other than "Crack Triangle."

The plaza was located in Clawson, across the street from the Hoover/Foster neighborhood. San Pablo Avenue formed the dividing line. Collectively, the neighborhoods were called Ghost Town—an umbrella designation that could also refer to the McClymonds neighborhood, which was bordered by Ralph Bunche, Prescott (also called Oakland Point), Dogtown (packs of semi-wild dogs were a feature), and the Lower Bottoms. No one knew what Ghost Town's real borders were; some held that they shifted, year by year and month to month, in a constant reflection of local gang activities. The name was a mystery, as well. Some thought that it had to do with the neighborhood's funeral parlors, or with the coffin-building companies that had operated, side by side, on Filbert Street, two blocks down from the future home of the East Bay Rats' clubhouse. Others believed that it dated back to the 1950s and 1960s, when West Oakland neighborhoods experienced sharp population drops, or to the drug wars of the late 1980s and early 1990s, when Oakland's homicide rate spiraled out of control. One theory held that Ghost Town was a corruption of "Holy Ghost Town" and referenced the neighborhood's churches: Apostolic Bible Way Church, Olivet Institutional Missionary Baptist Church, Miraculous Word Christian Center, Living Word Ministries Community Church, New Christian Fellowship Missionary Baptist Church, Lighthouse Mission Center Church of God in Christ, Market Street Seventh-day Adventist Church—the list of names went on like a litany. There were no supermarkets in West Oakland, no chain stores, movie theaters, or cemeteries. But just down from the clubhouse, a single block was home to St. Mark's Missionary Baptist Church, Solid Foundation Baptist Church, True Missionary Baptist Church, and the West Street Baptist Church. Most of the churches were small, some were tiny, but there were dozens of them: storefront churches with hand-painted signs; churches run out of old movie theaters, old supermarkets, and homes; churches that occupied stand-alone structures of less determinate purpose. Their cumulative effect was profoundly dispiriting.

"Oakland is depressing," Huey P. Newton had written in a memoir called *Revolutionary Suicide*. "It resembles a ghost town, but a ghost town with actual inhabitants."

Newton had grown up nearby, in a two-story house on Forty-seventh Street. He'd gone on to lead the Black Panther Party, which had once been headquartered in West Oakland, and published *Revolutionary Suicide* in between murder trials, in 1973. I read the book in a Penguin Classics edition published in 2009: the Panthers had come up in the world, albeit posthumously, and some of the neighborhoods they had patrolled had become respectable, too. The Fifty-seventh

Street bungalow where Newton and Bobby Seale had formed the Black Panthers in 1966 was one case in point: it was sold by Seale's family, not long after my move to Oakland, then sold again—flipped for double the amount (and ten times the price that Seale's parents had paid for it in 1960)—a few months later. "People move," Seale would say when reporters came calling. "Humans move. Power to the people, whether they're black, white, blue, whatever."

Seale himself had moved to the suburbs, to El Sobrante, in Contra Costa County. Families from many of Oakland's African American communities were moving to places like El Sobrante, or Antioch, or San Leandro, an East Bay suburb that had once employed police officers to turn blacks back at its border. Across the bay, in San Francisco, historically black neighborhoods like the Fillmore had undergone multiple waves of gentrification; prohibitively expensive, the city had become a playground for venture capitalists, engineers, and software developers. Just north of Ghost Town, Emeryville—which had once been the site of paint factories, petroleum refineries, slaughterhouses, sewage runoffs, speakeasies, gambling parlors, and bordellos—had also changed beyond recognition. During the Depression, Earl Warren, then the district attorney for Alameda County, had called Emeryville "the rottenest city on the Pacific Coast." Fifty years later, police chief John LaCoste, who'd inherited the job, and de facto control of Emeryville, from his father, could still be found running the city's business from his table at the Townhouse Bar and Grill, which had once been the speakeasy next door to Chubby Turner's brothel. Now, Emeryville was home to IKEA and the local Apple Store, to companies like Pixar and Electronic Arts, and to a vocational school, called Ex'pression College for Digital Arts, that ran in shifts, on a 24-7 schedule, to feed the local demand for CGI animators and video game designers. Emeryville was just up the street from Ghost Town

(Pixar's campus was a three-minute drive from Saint Andrews Plaza), tiny (1.2 square miles), packed, and booming with industry. Ten percent of the population lived in freestanding houses, two hundred of which remained. The rest lived in lofts and condominiums, many of which were located inside of actual shopping malls. But, despite its proximity to Emeryville, Ghost Town was not packed or booming. By all outward appearances, it had not changed at all, except to empty out and wither. Here, and elsewhere in the city, Oakland still looked like the place that Huey P. Newton—who'd been gunned down, in West Oakland, in 1989—had known.

I settled a few miles away, in a wealthier North Oakland neighborhood, in a bungalow around the corner from Cole Coffee, which I'd remembered as one of the East Bay Rats' regular hangouts. The Rats were still there, sitting on milk crates, smoking, and shooting the shit on the sidewalk across the street from the café. I saw them there the first time I drove past. But I didn't recognize any I'd met, and decided that it would be best to wait for Trevor to make the introductions. When I heard from him, a few days later, it was via text message.

"Dirtbag," he'd written.

I replied with a few question marks.

"Dirtbag Challenge meet me there."

I texted back my okay.

The Dirtbag Challenge took place, every fall, in Hunters Point, San Francisco, on the last, dead-end block of Quesada Avenue. The rules of the challenge were simple: contestants were given one month to build motorcycles (the eponymous "dirtbags") that would weather a hundred-mile ride, at a cost of less than one thousand dollars. Some of the bikes that they'd built went beyond the basic requirements: they had ape hanger handlebars, stretched gas tanks, and names like Naughty Lady and Bad Bitch II. But most of the dirtbags were made out of plumbing fixtures, old car parts, or bicycle parts, and many bore a familial resemblance to Rat bikes.

Although they had not invented it, the Dirtbag Challenge was a perfect distillation of the Rats' own, ersatz *Mad Max* aesthetic. The crowd looked like the crowds that a fight night would draw. The scene was the color of speed metal, smoke, and black leather. Even the word "dirtbag"—a term of disparagement, turned on its head—was Rat-like, in ways that reminded me of the East Bay Rats' origin story, as it had been told to me, during my first trip to Oakland, by Trevor's friend Everett Moore.

Everett had been an original club member; he'd even come up with the club's name, for which he'd been awarded a case of beer. Everett had meant the name as a sort of joke. But, from the get-go, Trevor had taken it seriously.

"Trevor always wanted to do things the right way," Everett had told me. "He wanted to make sure that we had no conflicts with the serious, established clubs. So, one day, he and I went down to a shop the Hells Angels had, across the street from their clubhouse in Oakland. We must have been teenagers, the first time we walked in there. In retrospect, it was really stupid. But we did walk in there, and Trevor came up to their main guys. He was really forthright. He said, 'We want to form a club, and we'd like to have your sign-off on that.' The Angels said, 'What's it called, your club?' Trevor told them. And the Angels said, 'What the fuck? Why would you call yourself a Rat? Why don't you just call yourselves East Bay Finks?' You know, 'rat' is a jailhouse term. It means 'snitch.' The Angels, man, they were laughing at us, laughing at our name—they thought we were idiots, and maybe we were. But in the end they said, 'You have our blessing,' which was all Trevor had really wanted from them. That was a big day for us."

I did not see any Hells Angels at the challenge. But the Soul

Brothers, Ravens, and Unknowns were there, along with members of the San Francisco Motorcycle Club, which had formed in 1904 (making it the second-oldest motorcycle club in the country), admitted women in 1910 (ten years before women were given the vote), and, in the years leading up to the First World War, counted the mayor of San Francisco among its members. I saw motorcycle collectors, who'd brought antique bikes to show off, and stunt riders who raced up and down Quesada Avenue, or reared up on their rear wheels and spun in place, pulling their bikes up impossibly high on their balance points. Hundreds of people were there when I arrived, and the crowd grew larger as the day wore on. It was the biggest gathering of bikers I'd seen, there was a lot to take in, and it took me some time to locate the Rats.

When I did see them, they were huddled around a weird, one-wheeled machine that had once been some sort of motorcycle. Now, the machine had skids, an engine, and handlebars, which were attached to a wooden platform that rested on the ground. There was a rope tied to the back of the platform, and a tire tied to the end of the rope, and when the Rats' huddle broke, a man with a rat skull tattooed on his own skull stepped over the rope and onto the platform. With one hand on the handlebars, he started the engine, which turned a few times before catching, giving a second Rat just enough time to run out, douse the tire in gasoline, and light a match. The crowd moved back as that Rat set the tire on fire. Then the first Rat took off, making wide, awkward turns at both ends of the block before racing back down to his starting point. Black smoke poured out from the tire, which had melted, halfway, into the pavement. The crowd was cheering. But I saw that the Rat with the rat skull tattoo was scowling and that the other Rats—there were eight or nine of them—were scowling, too.

A few of the Rats looked familiar. Trevor was standing a few yards away. But, somehow, the day's mood had soured, and when I waved to Trevor he seemed to ignore me and turned toward J.T., the Rats' treasurer, who had put on his helmet and climbed onto one of the bikes. J.T. rode a few yards, out into the street, stopped, and a few moments later another biker rode up beside him: J.J., the erstwhile lieutenant. It was the first time I'd seen J.J. since he'd been expelled from the club.

They stayed in the street, the Rat and the ex-Rat, glaring and rocking their bikes back and forth. They were close, almost touching, and the crowd stopped cheering—nobody moved—though I could hear whispers from people half hoping for bad, bloody things to start happening. If they did, I wondered, would someone there intervene? I glanced at Trevor, who glanced back and shrugged, acknowledging me at last. J.T. revved his engine, and J.J. revved his. Then J.J. peeled off and raced up the strip, J.T. shot off after him, and the rest of the Rats melted into the crowd, leaving me there, trying to understand what I'd seen.

CHAPTER SIX

It took more than a few conversations with Trevor, the Rats, and other interested parties before I could begin to make sense of the story, which, despite all the drama with J.J., was that of a very fast club that had slowed to a not-quite standstill.

For one thing, Trevor had played down the number of children that the Rats had had since my last visit, and the effect that those children had had on the club. Biker dads tended to take better care of themselves—to drink less and ride more carefully. They had less time to spend with the club. Rats and ex-Rats who had looked and acted like overgrown adolescents during my first visit to Oakland had gotten day jobs, bought houses, and bikes that were newer and nicer than Rat bikes. They answered to wives, ex-wives, and baby mamas. J.J. still lived in Oakland's Lower Bottoms but now had a daughter with Casey, the woman who'd once gone with Norton Aaron Fuller, and had been an immediate cause of J.J.'s expulsion from the club. Aaron's brother, Davey Fuller, had moved out of Oakland entirely: he lived in Concord now, with two little girls of his own, and was going to school to become a counselor for soldiers with PTSD. Several other Rats had also moved away, dropped out of the club, or simply lost interest. Norton Aaron had been the most outgoing Rat, a natural ambassador for the club. After his death, the club's rate of recruitment had dropped below its attrition rate. By the time of the challenge, the Rats were down to a single prospect, named Caleb, who had his own kid to raise and not enough time to devote to the club. A few months later, Caleb dropped out as well.

The Rats I'd met before had all changed, and, to me, it seemed that Trevor was losing his grip on the club. He was drinking more heavily, dating erratically—he'd sworn off the Korean girls he'd been dating when we first met, and was now seeing, mostly, Latinas. ("Mexicans are like methadone for Asian girls," he explained.) To the exclusion of most other things, he, too, had become obsessed with children. He wanted kids of his own, to hunt with and homeschool—he wanted lots of them—and he spent much of his time and his energy thinking and talking about them, in ways that turned out to be self-defeating. Trevor had become a local celebrity. He had no trouble attracting women. But he would talk about kids on the very first date, which did not lead him to have many second dates, while the club, which was the family he already had, suffered from his neglect. "I'd step down," he told me, "if I thought there was someone who'd do a good job in my place."

From time to time, other Rats did try to fill Trevor's vacuum. There were squabbles as a result, and arguments over Trevor's continued occupancy of the clubhouse, which most of the Rats thought of (and not without reason) as theirs to do whatever they wanted with. Trevor kept an eye out but followed the management strategy that he'd picked up from books and documentaries about the Second World War. "Hitler had issues," he told me. "But then he'd hang back and let his generals fight it out among themselves."

As a management style, this seemed to me to have its limitations.

The Rats still hosted fight nights. Once in a while, another sofa or piano got burned out on the San Pablo median strip. But the fun had begun to go out of such things. At the clubhouse, Nate's vest hung, behind glass, next to Norton Aaron's. The burned-out prow of a miniature Viking ship the Rats had used to launch Aaron's ashes hung from the ceiling. There were gaps, now, on the walls where old pictures of J.J. had hung, and pictures of him under laminate, on the clubhouse bar, had all been x-ed out, or covered with stickers that read: NORTON R.I.P. Out in the yard, NORTON R.I.P. had been painted on one of the walls, and in the Berkeley hills, on a low wall where bikers gathered, I'd seen the same thing—NORTON R.I.P. spray painted in big black letters. When I'd first met them, the Rats had been young and relatively carefree. Now, as they neared middle age, they had surrounded themselves with reminders of their own mortality.

"There were different chapters to the club's history," Davey Fuller told me.

"At first," he said, "the Rats lived in squats and warehouses. Did whatever it took to survive. Then there was an influx. In came us brothers, along with all of the war veterans. That's when we got the sense that our club was bigger than the sum of its parts. The feeling lasted for five years or so. But if Altamont was the end of the Summer of Love, then Nate's death was the end of our own age of innocence."

Trevor put things more succinctly: "We thought that we were immortal," he said. "We truly thought we were invincible. We'd read all the stats. We knew what the odds were. But all of us had crashed and bounced back—broken legs and bounced back—we'd *always* bounced back. Until Nate's death, and Norton Aaron's, it really did seem like nothing bad would ever happen to us."

* * *

Norton Aaron had died in 2008, on a freeway overpass in Oakland. According to the coroner, he'd been moving at sixty-five miles per hour when he'd gone off of his motorcycle and hit a concrete pillar—head-on—hard enough to crack his helmet in half, while his motorcycle traveled for a few more yards. Oddly, the bike was all but undamaged. But it's more than likely that Aaron was dead by the time it came to a stop.

"Aaron died instantly," Davey told me, "like a bug hitting a windshield, and dropped down to the ground below. There's a Highway Patrol station right there, on Telegraph Avenue. A CHP officer was outside, smoking. He heard the crash, put out his cigarette, and called it in. Then he drove up onto the overpass and saw the motorcycle. When he looked over the edge, he saw a body, right back down by where he had been standing."

Other Rats told me that J.J. had gone around town, after Norton Aaron's death, talking shit, telling people that Aaron had had it coming. He'd gone to the tattoo parlor, the coffee shop. "He was at Cole Coffee the *day* Aaron died, mean mugging us," Davey said.

The Rats brought up strange details: the clean condition of Norton Aaron's bike; the fact that he'd been wearing only one glove, and that his phone had gone missing. (If Aaron *had* stopped on the side of the road, had he removed a glove to make a phone call? If so, wouldn't this have made him an easy target?) They alluded to all the bad blood between J.J. and the Fuller brothers—a story that seemed to involve several women and was so convoluted that I gave up trying to unravel it. What was clear was that years had gone by with J.J. and the Rats at each other's throats—an unsustainable, poisonous atmosphere. The encounter I'd seen at the challenge had been bad enough. But what if the same sort of thing were to happen at night, out on a road with no witnesses? Several

Rats told me it already had; that J.J. had buzzed them, out on the roads, come up behind them, riding too fast and too close, on several occasions. If he'd done it to them, who could say what had happened with Norton Aaron?

A Rat named Jason Lockwood told me that, at first, he'd taken the gossip about J.J. with a grain of salt. "What it looks like," he said, "is that a car hit Aaron and, sad and awful as that is, kept going. Norton was dressed in black, on an unlit overpass. It's a human body against metal. It was probably a random hit-and-run." But on a long weekend—the Fourth of July—Jason had gone into the hills, and up to the wall where NORTON R.I.P. had been painted. "My girlfriend and I were hanging out, talking, and J.J. was there," he recalled. "He and I had yelled at each other, maybe once. That had ended with him saying, 'I don't want to talk to you anymore.' So I'd figured things had blown over. I was really surprised when we pulled away, and went through a turn, and J.J. dipped into the turn with us. It was like we were racing on a track. Okay, whatever, sometimes you do make a pass in the hills. But when we got down to the bottom I heard a motor revving behind us. J.J. had been waiting there, waiting to buzz us in traffic. In the end, he just brushed us. But it was so weird, so bizarre. And with a girl on the back of my bike, I think that it was a bit extra-shitty. Why would you involve another human being?"

For Jason, that encounter raised serious questions about J.J.'s character—which, Jason told me, was that of an overgrown bully.

"Some would say that J.J.'d tried to capitalize on the idea that people thought he *had* killed Norton, to make him seem even scarier and bigger than he is; that he did it with his little road rage tricks. I don't know that for a fact, and I was a big proponent of J.J.'s right on up until the time where he did it to me. But I'll have casual conversations, now, and find out about other shitty stuff he's done. It's amazing to me: how did I never know any of this before? The reason, I found out, is that he was a Rat. Everyone had his back. Who was going to talk about him? He's got all these guys around him—he's a perfectly dangerous individual on his own—but it's even worse when no one will talk about it because he's with us."

I heard similar stories from Davey Fuller, and from a few other Rats. But even from Trevor's perspective, the Rats hadn't always been blameless. "J.J. had been staring all day, on the day of the Challenge," he said. "He'd been mad-dogging us like crazy. But J.T. was drunk, and instead of letting it go, J.T. tore off after him, hammered. Right after that, he showed up at the clubhouse, hammered. J.T. said that J.J. had tried to run him off the road. I said, 'I saw you take after him. Maybe he did try to run you off the road. But I know what kind of headspace you were in. I know how angry you were. And I know you're hammered right now, as you're trying to tell me the story.'

"As the club's president, who am I supposed to believe?" Trevor said. "What am I supposed to do? If J.T. and J.J. got into it, out on the freeway, then fine. That's fucking dangerous, but don't play the victim with me."

There was no happy ending that I could foresee. I was curious to hear J.J.'s side of the story. But the Rats were like a herd of dinosaurs—once they had settled upon a direction, they had no turning radius at all—and, like Trevor, I saw them bent on their course.

"J.J., J.T., either one of them could have died," I said.

"Exactly," said Trevor.

CHAPTER SEVEN

There once were dinosaurs in California. Giant fish, where the ground was still covered with water, ancient whales, mastodons, saber-toothed tigers. The first people appeared toward the end of the Paleolithic era, a little more than ten thousand years ago. When the Spanish arrived, in our sixteenth century, three hundred thousand lived on or in from the coast.

The Spanish barely bothered with colonization. There were the missions, where Indians worked as indentured servants, and ranchos on land grants issued by Spanish governors, but the population of Spanish *Californios* never rose above 8,000, while the number of indigenous people dropped—to 150,000 at the time of American annexation in 1848, and 30,000 or so by the end of the gold rush in the 1850s.

For the Spanish, annexation was an economic disaster. In the East Bay, the old soldier and Indian fighter Luís María Peralta had presided over an enormous, 44,800-acre land grant he'd called Rancho San Antonio. This was the country that present-day Oakland, Berkeley, Emeryville, Albany, Alameda,

Piedmont, and San Leandro would all be founded upon, and toward the end of his rather long life Peralta divided it among his sons, who were instructed to live in accord, without avarice, and to be mindful of each other's cows. "Inasmuch as the land is narrow," Don Luís wrote in his will, "it is indispensable that the cattle should become mixed up, for which reason I command my sons to be friendly and united."

There were no stores or hotels on Rancho San Antonio. For most purposes there was no money; in those days cowhides were called "California dollars." In the hills, redwoods stood so high in groves that ship's captains on the far side of the bay employed them as navigational reference points. The flatlands were covered in clover and thick with oaks, and so many birds nested down by the water that hunters boasted of bringing several down with one shot. American rule brought the first American settlers—the Patten brothers, who'd sailed forth from Boston, and Moses Chase, who seemed to have boiled the whole story of Exodus down to the three syllables of his name. They negotiated leases with the Peraltas and lived peacefully on their land. But Chase and the Pattens were followed by American squatters, foremost among them a trio of men, named Edson Adams, Horace Carpentier, and Andrew Moon, who ended up running the city of Oakland.

Along with his partners, Carpentier helped himself to nearly five hundred acres of Peralta land, divided that land into lots, and leased the lots to other squatters, many of whom were Americans who'd tried their luck in the gold fields, failed, and taken up other pursuits. Because the land never had belonged to the partners, none of the leases were legal. Nonetheless, a town was incorporated, in 1852, and reincorporated, in 1854, as a city. That year, following a contest in which he claimed more votes than the city had voters, Carpentier was elected as Oakland's first mayor.

Carpentier was a young lawyer from Galway, New York.

(Moon and Adams were from Binghamton, New York, and Fairfield, Connecticut, respectively.) A few years earlier he'd graduated, top of his class, from Columbia College. But by most accounts, he'd already become a poor advertisement for his profession. Sometimes, it was said, he would dress like a priest and say the rosary with Spanish families he was then defrauding. Sometimes, having gained a family's trust, he'd represent them in court cases in which he himself was the opposing party. A suit that the Peraltas filed against the squatters went all the way up to the United States Supreme Court—which confirmed the family's claim in 1856, by which time Oakland's redwoods had all been cut down and taxes and lawyer's fees had greatly reduced the Peraltas' holdings.

In the meanwhile, Horace Carpentier had managed to get all of Oakland's waterfront signed over to himself, for a period of thirty-seven years, in exchange for five dollars, a promise to build three wharves and a schoolhouse, and 2 percent of the wharfage fees he collected. In one of his first acts as mayor, he'd amended those terms and come to own the waterfront outright. Several times, Oakland's squatters revolted against him. On at least one occasion, Carpentier rowed out into the bay, waited out the rioting, returned, and sued the city for damages. In 1855, he was finally ousted from office, though not his position of power, and the "Battle of the Waterfront" (as the city's attempt to regain control came to be known) lasted for more than five decades.

Throughout his career, Carpentier was a close associate of San Francisco's political boss, David Broderick. And yet, as it grew, Carpentier's city came to define itself in opposition to Broderick's. If San Francisco was anarchic and free-for-all—prototypically Western—Oakland would present itself as orderly, bourgeois, Northeastern in feel and flavor. Almost from the moment of its founding, it impressed visitors as a place where the people in charge had long since agreed upon their interests. "Oakland is the Staten Island of the bay region," the poet and traveler Bayard Taylor wrote, just four years after the city's incorporation. "Here the shore rises in gentle undulations, its prevailing tawny hue forming a mellow background for the thick, dark, green forms of the venerable oak trees. Steamboats, piers, warehouses, cottages, gardens, orchards, fenced fields, roads striking off into the country, carts laden with produce, horsemen, fishing boats, omnibuses, stages, were among the features which suggested age and long established order." But the semblance of order was just that: a semblance. If Bayard Taylor had known the place better, he would have described it as San Francisco's dueling ground.

In 1852, a San Francisco alderman named John Cotter fought a duel with John Nugent, editor of the *San Francisco Herald*, with David Broderick serving as one of the alderman's seconds.* Both men survived, but in 1854 Colonel Deveraux Woodlief, of Texas, was shot dead by Achilles Kewan, who met his own end several years later while fighting with William Walker (another *San Francisco Herald* editor, and a celebrated duelist in his own right) during Walker's quixotic attempt to take over Nicaragua. "After this," in Oakland, noted another contemporary, "dueling became so common that the report of one would attract no more attention than the announcement of a cocking main or a dog fight."

Alongside the duels and the cockfights and dogfights were bullfights in a ring the Peraltas had built—these were outlawed in 1854—and bear-baiting contests. At night, gangs of San Franciscans rowed across the bay and tried to jump local land claims; in Oakland, the melees that ensued were called "jumper riots." And, of course, there were the squatter riots, along with de rigueur knife fights and the lynching of cattle thieves. Years

---

*In 1859, Broderick succumbed to dueling wounds sustained just outside of San Francisco, at Lake Merced. In 1889 his opponent, David Terry—a former chief justice of the Supreme Court of California—was shot dead by a federal marshal.

later, discrimination against the Chinese became widespread and violent. And yet, in Oakland, the semblance of order remained—if anything, it solidified, during the decades that followed—until, like a prop, it collapsed.

Now here we were, in the ruins.

CHAPTER EIGHT

This neighborhood in West Oakland, most people call it Dogtown. It used to be a very crime-ridden area. My house was raided by the ATF, FBI—numerous task force agencies—before I recycled. They looked on me for suspicion of homicide, manufacturing methamphetamines, stealing cars. . . . I'm going to tell you right now, recycling not only saved my life but my girlfriend was working on the street as a prostitute. She no longer has to do that because of recycling. As far as I'm concerned, if you take away the recycling center crime will rise again in Oakland—worse than you could ever think. I don't want to go to jail. I'm sick and tired of going to jail. And until I can get a job in Oakland—until I can get a JOB—I think that you should let me recycle. All I'm doing is taking garbage.

—JASON DEWITT,
addressing Oakland's city council, March 9, 2009

On Bastille Day, July 14, 2010, Oakland police chief Anthony Batts announced that Oakland's police department would no longer respond to 911 calls regarding waste dumping, check kiting, vandalism, vehicular collisions, extortion, embezzlement, burglary, break-ins, identity theft, intentional poisoning, downed power lines, the presence of unregistered sex offenders—all in all, the chief listed forty-four crimes and complaints that Oakland's residents (those whose computers hadn't been stolen) would now have to register online. In effect, Batts was saying, the Oakland Police Department would only respond to violent crimes in progress. In reality, he was describing a worst-case scenario that had already come to pass.

The announcement made national headlines; locally, it was greeted with shrugs. But the Rats' ears pricked up at the news that Oakland's cops would no longer come out for noise complaints.

Like criminals, they were unusually attuned to dips in civic awareness, and always ready to take full advantage. In a sense, the club was almost a form of self-awareness on the city's part: Oakland's consciousness, if not its conscience. And so, a few days after Chief Batts's announcement, the Rats dragged an armchair out onto the San Pablo median strip, doused it with gasoline, and set a fire, which had all but gone out by the time that a fire truck pulled up in front of the clubhouse. A police car drove past and slowed, without stopping, and later that night, when the rest of the Rats had gone home, Trevor took a rifle out, put a bull's-eye up on an overturned table, and fired off ten or twelve rounds.

This time the cops didn't come around at all.

The Rats conducted other experiments out on the strip: burned sofas, motor scooters, an upright piano. One day, they filled a shopping cart with empty beer cans, strung it up between two poles that they'd greased with engine oil, and took bets on how long it would take before the cans disappeared. "Crackheads are ingenious," said Trevor, correctly—days later, the cans were all gone. But no one knew how the recyclers had managed it, because the shopping cart was still hanging there, empty, in front of the clubhouse, high up above San Pablo Avenue. This was so surprising that it took the Rats a few days to lose interest and turn their attentions toward fight parties.

Throughout the years, fight parties had been the Rats' most consistent rallying mechanisms and recruitment machines. And yet, it had been a long time since they'd hosted one. In a roundabout way, the neighborhood recycling center was to blame.

The shopping-cart people who hung around the center pilfered cans and bottles from city recycling bins. Sometimes they broke into houses and stole pipes and plumbing fixtures. Just that year, they'd broken into the clubhouse, which must have taken some courage. Now, the Rats' shower (which was also Trevor's own, personal shower) no longer worked.

People who lived close to the center would show up at city council meetings, complaining about piss-soaked sidewalks in front of their homes, piles of human feces, drug dealers who serviced the trade, and the sound of breaking bottles: recyclers were paid by the pound, they explained, and some of them seemed to believe that piles of broken glass actually weighed more than bags full of bottles. When the council tried to pass a resolution to curb the recycling center's activities, the center's owner bused forty recyclers down to city hall. They held up signs while he addressed the council or waited in line to make their own speeches, which tended to be vaguely threatening. A rumor went around that the owner had bribed his supporters with fried chicken dinners, which turned out not to have been the case—though he might have bought pizza and soda pop. Either way, the resolution had failed.

Afterward, Trevor told me, a council member had approached the Rats and asked for documentary evidence— photos or, better yet, videos—of illegal activities in and around the recycling center. But much as they disliked the recyclers, the Rats were more contemptuous of snitches. They'd refused the invitation, and from that point onward the cops had shown up to shut down their parties.

Now, Trevor reasoned, in the wake of Chief Batts's announcement, the Rats could throw bigger parties—intricate affairs, with themes that went way beyond the old "drunks versus stoners" paradigm. He tapped a series of ideas out into his iPhone:

"Punks vs. Hipsters."
"Gays vs. Straights."
"Butchers vs. Vegetarians."
"Jews vs. Gentiles."
"Brothers."

Soon, two Jews—one a club member, the other a friend—were trading blows in back of the clubhouse, prepping for a four-man fight against two Gentiles. The stakes were set at bragging privileges and the right to name the club's next holiday party, and flyers were printed to advertise the fight, which would be billed as "The Battle of the Sectses."

To come off properly, a fight night had to gather enough momentum to carry it through from nine or ten in the evening into the morning hours. In practice, this meant three or four fights an hour, for four or five hours on end. A solid draw, with spectators crammed around the ring and crowded up on the roof, looking down at the fights below them, would require dozens of fighters. To meet the demand, Trevor began to give boxing lessons, every Friday at the clubhouse, before the start of his shift at the Ruby Room. Equipment was minimal—two jump ropes, two sets of gloves, a heavy bag off in the corner—but the lessons were free, and Trevor was a patient, methodical instructor. Alone or in pairs, punks, hipsters, and heshers began to file through, train, and sign up for fight cards. I began to bring Lucy down to the training sessions. We'd jump rope, spar, or shadowbox. Our muscles would be sore for days. Afterward, we'd drive down to the Ruby Room, drink beer, and listen to Trevor talk about fighters he'd seen over the years.

Most had walked in off the street, Trevor said: strangers, who'd put on gloves, or boxed bare knuckled, for any number of rounds, against any number of opponents. They were combat vets or martial artists. Some were street fighters; others had fought in Golden Gloves tournaments or in prison. But the one who stuck in Trevor's memory had come around when the club was still in its infancy. He'd been a high school kid who'd shown up at one of the very first fight parties the Rats had thrown, and "sad" was the word Trevor used to describe him. In fact, his story was terrible.

"The parties were starting to get big," said Trevor.

The bartender poured us a first round of beer.

"I was living at J.J.'s place, down in the Lower Bottoms. People were boxing nonstop in our backyard. One day, our next-door neighbors yelled over the fence that someone wanted to come over. We said, 'Yeah, come over!' But the kid who came over looked real young to me. He wasn't big. But he was so gung ho, I asked him what gym he fought out of. The kid said, 'Oh, I don't fight out of a gym.' Then he beat the crap out of a grown-up. Fought with his hands down, like Roy Jones Jr., you know? He was a really good boxer, a natural. When he took the gloves off, I asked him again: 'No, really, where do you box out of?' The kid said, 'Really, nowhere, I just play football.'

"It turned out that the kid was sixteen. He looked a lot younger than that. He must have been a hell of a football player.

"Back then, in that part of the neighborhood, we knew all

of the gangsters. We knew everybody. It was actually safe, in a weird sort of way. People watched over our bikes while we slept; there wasn't a lot of transient crime. But one day I saw thirty guys out in the middle of the street. Two of them were fighting. One of them was the kid. He was beating the crap out of some grown-up. I was just walking home with a twelve-pack; I didn't know what was going on. Then I heard a shotgun go off. I thought, 'Fuck, I'm getting shot at!' But when I looked over, I saw one of the old-time gangsters firing in the air. He was doing it to run everybody off. It had nothing at all to do with me. But when I got home I heard more gunshots going off in front of our house. I ran outside with a gun. I still didn't know what was happening. And I saw someone lying out there, in the street. It was the kid. He'd been shot in the leg.

"You know, when you watch shows like *CSI*, people get shot, and then the cops come to pick up the casings. To do all sorts of stuff. But the cop that came by that day just rolled his window down, yelled, 'Everybody all right?' and drove away. You might think, 'I'm in Oakland. It's not *CSI*.' But you wouldn't think that a cop would drive by, roll his window down, and drive away. The kid was still right there, bleeding. And if that cop had gotten out of his car, if he'd done some minimal investigation, it might have stopped a lot of things from happening."

Trevor trailed off, lifted his pint glass, drained it. The bartender walked over and Trevor pushed the glass toward him.

"Yep," he said.

The Ruby Room was a licensed establishment in Oakland, even a venerable one. As a courthouse bar, it had served two-martini lunches to Earl Warren's lawyers. And, even now, it was a beautiful space; the red velvet walls and long, wooden counter would have been the envy of bartenders in any other city. But the Ruby Room was also a speakeasy: a smoking bar, in a city and state where smoking in bars was not legal. The bar was not out of the way. City hall was a few blocks up the street; the courthouse was still around the corner. The main entrance to the main branch of Oakland's public library faced the Ruby Room's front door. But if you wanted to play pool or sit down at a table, you had to put up with thick clouds of cigarette smoke that filled the back room. In that sense, the bar was also an object lesson in things that Oakland's civic leaders would and would not tolerate.

Now, the smokers were starting to filter in. A DJ set her equipment up in a booth by the back of the bar. In the back room, a pool player called "Stripes!," and Trevor continued his story.

"What did happen," said Trevor, "was that the kid had been playing a five-dollar craps game. The guy he was playing with grabbed for the money, and then the kid kicked his ass. Right there, in the street, where everyone saw it. The guy, who might have been twenty-two, twenty-three, he didn't have the ego to take an ass whooping from a sixteen-year-old kid. He came back with a gun. Shot the kid. That was the part I had heard, almost witnessed. But the craps shooter didn't leave town. What I heard later was that, instead of going to the hospital, the kid had gone home, gotten his own gun, gone to the craps shooter's block, pulled his hoodie back so that everyone in the street could have seen him, and shot the guy in the face—killed the craps shooter, and split. We never saw him again. But a few days later, the craps shooter's family came around. They shot and killed the kid's dad, this super-nice, hardworking dude who was always fixing cars out in his driveway. And then the kid's cousins came up, from Los Angeles. There was a very high probability that more people were going to die. But the cousins did not know the neighborhood. With the kid gone and the father dead, they didn't even know anyone *in* the neighborhood. So they left empty-handed, went back to Los Angeles. The kid got picked up later, trying to board a ship."

"A ship?"

"A cruise ship, back east. As if there's no warrant out for him, or some statute of limitations on murder."

"How long had he been free for?"

"A year? Maybe less. I hope he's been boxing in prison."

For Trevor, this was a typical Oakland story. "I liked the kid," he said. "I knew him, he was a good kid, and I was sorry that he went to prison. I knew his dad, too—a good guy. Obviously, they had an edge to them. The dad had an edge, taught the kid to fight, and did a good fucking job of it. But fuck it, the kid, it seems so pointless, at sixteen, to ruin your life. It goes to show that, in the ghetto, it's always lose-lose. If the kid hadn't stood up for himself, if he'd let himself get punked, he would have been ridiculed, in the neighborhood, for the rest of his life. But, by retaliating, he wrecked his whole life."

If anything about the story was unusual, it was that the kid was arrested at all, because Oakland had become an especially good place to get away with murder. In 2010 (the year of my arrival in Oakland), close to three-quarters of homicides went unsolved. All of the cops I was meeting would tell me that they were outmanned, outgunned, and demoralized. Other violent cities—Baltimore, Newark, Detroit—had forty or fifty cops for every ten thousand residents. In Oakland, the number was closer to fifteen or sixteen. Shootings, killings, armed robberies, and rapes were daily occurrences.

Half the size of San Francisco, Oakland had its own airport, a zoo, and three major-league sports teams. It had the fifth-largest port in America. And, unlike beleaguered American cities it might have resembled statistically, Oakland had pockets of tremendous affluence—not even pockets, but entire neighborhoods. Piedmont, which was surrounded on all sides by Oakland, was its own civic entity, with its own police force, excellent schools, and villas that would not have been out of place on the Italian Riviera. In the twenties, Piedmont had been known as the "City of Millionaires." It still was a city of millionaires—in Oakland, I'd heard it described as "an island of paranoia, surrounded by its own worst fears"—but, in the previous decade, there had been no murders in Piedmont, three reported rapes, and fifteen assaults. If you had the resources, it was perfectly possible to live in Piedmont, or in the Oakland Hills, or in one of the city's other wealthy neighborhoods, take BART to work in San Francisco, and remain blissfully ignorant of Oakland's crime rate (although, in practice, this might have been harder to do in the hills, which doubled as dumping grounds for dead bodies). But, by the same token, there were people down in the meat-grinder flats of East or West Oakland who'd never set foot in Piedmont, who'd barely seen San Francisco, who did not know the ocean, a few miles away.

It struck me that, at the least, the kid in Trevor's story had tried to see the ocean.

For me, the story was doubly instructive. It described the way violence could spiral outward: from kid to craps shooter, and on to the father, and then the kid's cousins. But it was also a story about containment: like a conflagration in a closed space, the killings had burned themselves out.

Trevor, the Rats, and the kids who showed up for Friday night boxing went through dozens of beers in the course of a session. They drank Bud and Bud Lights and tossed the empties out onto the sidewalk in front of the clubhouse. Without fail, the cans would all be gone by the time each session was over. Sometimes, you'd catch glimpses of the shopping-cart people as they bent over to gather the cans, or hear them squabbling outside. Once in a while you'd hear explosions off in the distance: gunshots, firecrackers—I couldn't tell the sounds apart. Mostly, the street was still, and much quieter than a city street should be. One Friday, I came to the clubhouse early and found Trevor alone at the bar, lost in thought, listening to Merle Haggard on Pandora. "I'm a lonesome fugitive," he said as I sat down beside him. Later, when the room filled up, he switched over to the Ramones.

The boxing ring in back of the clubhouse left just enough room for a barbecue pit and Trevor's Rat truck, an old, black Land Cruiser, parked up against a wall on which somebody had spray-painted the words: NORTON R.I.P. Inside the club, two punk rock kids alternated between jumping rope and shadow-boxing while Trevor helped a woman named Bean with her form. "Jab!" he'd say, and hold his hands up as Bean stomped forward with her right foot, employing the same motion you'd use to squash a bug on the floor, threw her fist out, and connected with his open palm. They'd repeat the motion dozens of times, then move on to left crosses, right crosses, body blows, uppercuts.

"Right foot forward, slide with your left!"

"Keep your hands up!"

"Move! Move! Keep moving!"

Trevor and Bean would fall into a rhythm, neatly in sync with the Ramones, and keep at it for a minute or two before switching to a different exercise. I watched them from the bar. After a while, Trevor's friend Paul, who worked as a lawyer, came and sat down beside me. Then one of the Rats rode up and parked his bike up on the sidewalk. When the biker walked inside, Trevor broke off to introduce us.

"Timmers is going to fight with the Gentiles," he said.

Timmers was built like a pit bull, with a thick beard, hair that he'd slicked back with industrial-strength pomade, and a string of Hebrew letters tattooed on the back of his neck.

"Want to spar?" Trevor asked.

He was talking to me.

Timmers was a few inches shorter than I was, but twenty pounds heavier. He'd been training for weeks for the fight. I don't know how Trevor convinced me to get in the ring.

"Go on," he said. "He won't hit you back. Will you, Timmers?"

"What's the point then?" said Timmers.

"Toughen you up."

Trevor turned to me.

"Hit him as much as you want," he said. "Hit him in the face. Go for his kidneys. Get in there. Go on."

"Really?" I said.

"My circus, my monkeys," said Trevor.

I got in there, trying to remember what Trevor had taught me. At first, I hit slowly, tentatively, following instructions that I had heard Trevor give Bean. Timmers stayed in a crouch, with his gloves pressed up to his cheekbones, and batted my punches away. "Hit him!" Trevor kept saying, but I couldn't find a way through. When I did connect, Timmers would cross his arms and shove me backward into the ropes. He did this repeatedly, until it became exhausting, and infuriating, and I began to hit harder. After a couple of minutes of this, Timmers spat his mouth guard out onto the floor.

"I could take you out with one punch," he said. "I could do better with both hands stuffed in my pockets. I could kill you if I wanted to."

"You really do have to hit him," said Trevor.

"I'm hitting him!"

"Hard!"

I leaned against the corner ropes.

"He'll get mad if you don't hit him," said Trevor.

"Might get mad either way," Timmers said.

I threw my gloves down, picked them back up again, put

them back on, and began hitting as hard as I could. From what I could tell, it didn't make much of a difference.

Bean wore a black-lace bustier to the fights, short-shorts, and a garter belt. She was small and nervous—she was in her twenties, but looked like a teenager—and bounced up and down, jangling the bangles that hung from the belt. She had been in the ring for a minute or more with no one in the crowd taking her up on the challenge, it was the evening's first fight, and the referee, Jason Lockwood, was shaking his head.

"We need a girl," Jason said. "We need a girl to fight this girl!"

A chant went up: "Girl fight! Girl fight! Girl fight! Girl fight!"

No one came out from the crowd.

Trevor, standing just outside of the ropes, leaned over and whispered to Jason: "Small dude," he said.

Lockwood nodded and turned toward the crowd.

"Small dude!" he shouted. A new chant went up: "Small dude! Small dude! Small dude! Small dude!"

Then the crowd parted. There was a boy standing on the far side of the ring. He had braces, a mop of brown hair that covered his face, and I could just make out the words on his powder-blue sweatshirt: REDWOOD HILLS PONY CLUB.

I climbed up onto the ring next to Trevor.

"He looks terrified," I said.

"Or excited," said Trevor.

"Barely pubescent."

"It might be the first time he touches a girl."

The boy brushed his hair away from his eyes, looked up at Bean and over toward Trevor. Then the crowd pushed forward and the boy found himself up against the far side of the ring.

Lockwood walked back to where we were standing.

"If he wins, he's beaten a girl up," said Trevor.

"If he loses," said Jason, "well, that's almost worse."

"True," Trevor said. "Little dude might as well go for it."

The boy climbed through the ropes, turned back to look at the crowd, and bent down to pick up a boxing glove.

Cheers broke out.

"Fuck her up!" someone shouted.

"Punch her in the womb!"

"Punch her in the titty!"

"Ready?" Lockwood asked.

The boy nodded and Lockwood began to count down.

The crowd counted backward in unison.

At "Three," Bean hopped out to the center of the ring and stuck her glove out for a fist bump. The boy cocked his arm instead, aiming at her temple. There were boos, and Bean swatted the punch away and fought back, bloodying the boy's nose. They struggled for a few seconds, fell into a clinch. Then Bean stumbled and fell on the ropes. The boy rushed after her. The crowd perked up.

The boy hit Bean in the face, in the side of her head, in her stomach. She collapsed, with one arm over the ropes, and slid to her knees. Now, the crowd started jeering. Someone yelled, "You hit a girl!" Someone else yelled, "You asshole!" When Bean stood up, she was punch-drunk.

The boy gave it everything he had. Bean jackknifed, and when she came back up he punched her, quickly, three times in the stomach, once in the face, and once more below the rib cage. Bean bent over again, and this time she stayed folded over. Trevor began to yell—"You hate your mother!"—and the crowd booed and hollered as Lockwood walked over to raise the boy's hand.

"We have a winner," he said.

Someone in the crowd yelled out, "You fucking loser!"

"Not bad," said Trevor, before wandering off toward the clubhouse.

Julio was from Milpitas, a South Bay town known for its car dealerships and Vietnamese restaurants, but he spoke with a Mexican accent and looked like a Mexican bandit. His shaved head resembled a cannonball that had somehow grown eyes, a nose, and Pancho Villa's mustache. He'd gotten engaged that very morning, gotten defiantly drunk, and when the main fight card began, he appeared ringside, ready to fight on the side of either the Jews or the Gentiles.

"We're good here," Jason Lockwood said, as he nudged Julio away from the ropes.

Timmers turned toward Trevor and me, spat his mouth guard into his glove, and said, "Mexicans think they can fight on either team." Behind him, Julio had already snuck back through the ropes.

Timmers was very strong—he worked out constantly at the YMCA in downtown Oakland—with a low center of gravity. Tyler, the Ruby Room bartender whom Timmers had partnered with, had reach, and two or three inches on everyone else in the ring. But, taken together, the Jews must have weighed close to five hundred pounds. Seth was a Rat—a sweet-tempered guy, but imposing. Dave was an ex-member of a larger club called the Soul Brothers. Both of them were bruisers, and everyone sensed that the fight would be good, if only Julio would get out of the ring.

Trevor stood against the back wall, just behind the ropes. I was beside him and Lucy had set up a few feet away, behind one of the corners, where there was less of a chance that a stray blow or body would land on her. Everyone yelled at Julio, who seemed not to hear us but finally did crawl back over the ropes. Then the Jews and the Gentiles locked arms and huddled, together with Jason. When the huddle broke Jason spread his arms, sending the fighters to their respective corners, and began to count down.

An art student was there with her camera, standing on Trevor's far side, shooting photographs for her senior thesis. "Only here would you see a fight between Jews and Gentiles," she said.

"Well, not only here," Trevor told her.

Discounting Julio, who was half in and half out of the ring and still trying to tag his way in, as if the fight were a wrestling match, there were five men inside the ropes, and all sorts of distractions outside it. I missed the first punch and tuned in to see Tyler swinging at Dave's head, and over it. Timmers already had Seth in a clinch and was hitting him hard when Jason went in to break them up. Trevor leaned toward me and said, "The plan is to tire Seth out. But that doesn't really work when the guy's so much bigger. He can just rest on you, and Dave's so fat, he can take lots of punches."

"Don't be fat!" Trevor yelled in Dave's direction.

On the far side of the ring, Tyler switched over to body blows. He landed four in succession, and Dave went into a crouch.

"Don't be fat!" Trevor yelled.

Then Timmers slipped away from Seth to hit Dave, several times, in the back of his head. With every blow, I thought, "Brain damage." But, in the moment, Dave simply looked dazed.

"Switch!" Trevor yelled at the fighters. Tyler looked up, and Seth was in front of him. Then Tyler was down on the canvas.

The crowd roared. The photographer screamed at the fighters.

"Go kikes!" she yelled.

"Go what?" said Trevor.

"Kikes," said the photographer. "Is it okay to say 'kikes'?"

"If you feel like you have to," said Trevor.

Tyler got up and got knocked down again. He made it through the first round but went down for a third time in the second, leaving Dave, who had mostly recovered, and Seth, who hadn't been hit much at all, to double up on Timmers. It could have been worse: everyone in the ring was winded, and for a moment it looked like the Gentiles could at least fight to a draw. But as the fight wore on, the Jews' weight advantage broke more and more in their favor. In the fifth round, they ended matters with a double knockout. "Kikes!" the art student screamed one last time as they posed for a valedictory photograph.

People kept fighting, inside of the ring, long after the Jews and Gentiles were done. Then, at some point, the violence began to spill outward. Inside the clubhouse I heard a tall, skinny guy with long hair say the wrong thing to John Firpo—the tall, menacing Rat who'd been riding the Rats' unicycle back at the Dirtbag Challenge.

Fighting ran in Firpo's family. In 1923 his great-grandfather, the Argentinian boxer Luis Ángel Firpo, had knocked Jack Dempsey out of the ring: if not for the referee, who gave a slow count, and a few sportswriters, who pushed Dempsey back through the ropes, Firpo would have become the world's first Latin American heavyweight champion. George Bellows had captured the moment in *Dempsey and Firpo*, the great American sports painting, which I had seen at the Whitney Museum. I'd watched the fight, too: the whole thing had been captured on film and was unbelievably savage, in exactly the way that Bellows had tried to articulate: "I don't know anything about boxing," the artist had said. "I am just painting two men trying to kill each other."

John Firpo had had Bellows's painting tattooed on his torso. Now, I watched him punch the stranger who'd said the wrong thing. A single blow was all that it took to put the man on the concrete.

This was a thing that the Rats did, for the bored and unstable, for masochists, or men who were eager to show off and prove themselves in some dumb way. There was no shame in getting beaten up by one of the Rats. Anyone could walk into the clubhouse, tell one of them off. They'd kick your ass immediately, without getting mad or taking things personally. They were not conflict averse. They wouldn't even gang up on you, necessarily. Beatdowns were like a community service that the Rats provided.

The stranger didn't take his personally. He got back on his feet and apologized; told Firpo that his mom had just died; that he'd been fucked up, at his wit's end, and had not meant to say anything at all. Now that he had, he was sorry.

"I'm sorry about your mother," said Firpo, as he guided the man out of the clubhouse. I followed them, walking past a man who was propped on a bike on the sidewalk, surrounded by empty beer cans. There must have been dozens of cans: an unusual bounty for the shopping-cart person standing a few feet away, just outside the party's perimeter. But it was a bad place for the recycler to be, and bad timing, because just then the man got up off his bike, staggered a few feet, and shoved the recycler, sending him spinning into a row of bikes that the Rats and their guests had parked in a line in front of the clubhouse.

The recycler seemed to spin in slow motion—I held my breath—and yet the bikes didn't go down, in the clichéd manner, like dominoes. Through some superhuman effort, the recycler steadied himself instead. He stood for a moment and looked at us, blankly, with one hand on the seat of a motorcycle. Then two Rats stepped off the sidewalk and hit him.

They knocked the man down to the pavement, kicked him and punched him and dragged him, by the scruff of his shirt, into the middle of San Pablo Avenue. The recycler scrambled back to his feet. They knocked him down again and again. "I need to go stop this," I said, out loud, to no one. But I didn't go, and when I did go, I didn't run, and by the time I'd gotten to where the Rats had dragged him, the man was no longer there. Somehow, he'd crawled over the median strip. On the far side of San Pablo he stood up, then fell over again. I heard an engine start. Then a Rat rode his bike around the median, up to the man. He rocked the bike back and forth, nudging with his front tire, rolled back a few feet, gunned the engine, and rode his bike over the recycler's body.

I turned away. I wished that I'd turned away sooner. When I turned back, I expected to see something terrible. But there was nothing to see. The recycler was gone. The street was empty. And though we stayed at the clubhouse for another half hour or more, the police did not come around.

CHAPTER NINE

"Crackheads are surprisingly resilient," Trevor said a few days later, at the Ruby Room.

"I should have done something," I said.

"You could have," said Trevor. "All it takes is someone to say, 'Stop!'"

At the time, it hadn't even occurred to me.

"I didn't do anything."

"I wouldn't worry about it," said Trevor. "What's worse is what happened after you left. Almost everyone had gone home, almost, but at some point, four or five in the morning, Bean's friend Katie walked into the clubhouse."

"Katie from boxing lessons?"

"Yep. She walked in very slowly. Covered in blood, like Carrie at the prom. A minute later, Julio came in—chasing her, following her, we didn't know. The two of them had been around the corner, leaned up against our back fence."

Katie was a quiet girl in punk rock drag. She wasn't much bigger than Bean.

"We tried to figure out what happened," Trevor said. "Julio's excuse was that they were making out; I guessed his fiancée had gone home. He told us that he'd choked Katie out because she asked him to. That she had fallen and hit her head on the sidewalk. But Katie told us that when she woke up, Julio was trying to fuck her. The worst part was that her cheekbone was broken.

"We worked Julio over. We were punching him, kicking him. The whole time I was like, 'Wow, I really liked you, dude.' And then Paul, my friend, the lawyer, kept trying to jump in."

"The lawyer?"

"My lawyer. But he didn't know what the fuck he was doing, so we'd pull Paul off and go back to Julio. We held his legs apart. We kicked him in the balls. He was so drunk, he kept hobbling back up. I hit him with my carabiner—a D ring—as good as brass knuckles. Usually, that would knock someone out. Julio looked at me like a dog who didn't know why I'd decided to kick it. I was really surprised. So surprised, I let him walk away. But when he was half a block down, I got a shovel and started after him. I wanted to break his legs. One of the other guys stopped me. He really liked Julio, too.

"I was super-bummed about it. The police hadn't shown up at all. They still haven't arrested Julio. And the fact he's walking around now really upsets me. He's a former marine, which makes his hands deadly weapons. All of us knew he'd had issues with domestic violence. But we all thought he was taking lessons for that. Now I wish we had beaten him more, not left anything over."

At some point, I recalled, Katie and Bean had shown up at the clubhouse with their own homemade patches, both of which read: EAST BAY CATS. For the bikers, they were like mascots; from time to time, one of them would go with one of the Rats, but all of the Rats were protective of them. Julio had crossed a serious line. Just then, I didn't think I would see him again.

Julio wasn't the only one with a drinking problem. The bar was where Trevor was every night, and in the weeks that followed I met him there most nights, talked to him and the Rats, and to friends of the Rats', to cops and bartenders and other bikers, setting their best stories down in my notebook. Sometimes they'd ask questions about my work, which did not seem at all like work to them. Sometimes, the conversations went off on weird tangents. But most of the time, when enough had been drunk, things would circle around to Nate's absence, and Norton Aaron's. At the Ruby Room, Nate and Norton were still present, and the stories that I heard about Norton Aaron tended to be especially good. The best one I heard came from Paul, the lawyer.

Paul was a single dad who rode a bike, drank, and hung out with the Rats at Cole Coffee. He showed up, and sometimes fought, at the fight nights. From time to time, he represented the Rats in court cases. One night, he told me about representing Norton Aaron: "Aaron was heading home to Concord. He was on his motorcycle, coming from a bar in Oakland just after two a.m., which is the time that bars close in California. He went through the Caldecott Tunnel on Highway 24, which is the dividing line between Alameda County and Contra Costa County, and a place where the California Highway Patrol often set up and wait to find people speeding. The police report that I read later estimated Aaron's speed when he came out of the tunnel as well over a hundred miles per hour. A parked police car started after him, but even accelerating beyond a hundred and forty m.p.h. was not able to catch up to him for the ten or so miles it takes to get from the tunnel to the 24/680 interchange, at the city of Walnut Creek.

"Aaron told me (attorney-client privilege does not really apply, as Aaron is now deceased) that he didn't realize the cops were behind him until he was about halfway to the interchange. But when he saw the lights, he figured he had to make a run for it. At the time, he had an open application with the Oakland Police Department—I believe he'd even taken some tests and had an interview, all of which were positive toward him getting a job as a police officer. And so, he ran.

"The problem is, while a motorcycle has no trouble outrunning a car, it's not so easy to outrun a radio. Somewhere toward Walnut Creek the second and third units picked him up, were waiting for him as he came down the freeway. At the 24/680 interchange, Aaron headed north toward Concord. By this time there were at least four police cars chasing him, both CHP and Walnut Creek PD.

"Aaron exited the freeway in Concord, where he lived and where he knew the streets. Now Concord PD got involved, bringing the total number of police cars chasing to six. All the while, Aaron is running red lights and stop signs and riding, at breakneck speeds, down residential streets. His first attempt to shake them was driving through a park. He lost the guys closest to him and got picked up by the guys farther away, who were able to divert and get to the other side of the park just as he was exiting.

"At this point, there are more Concord PD and Highway Patrol involved, and they're blocking off roads trying to contain Aaron. The chase has been going on for over fifteen minutes. Longer, even, if you start from where the first car picked up just after the tunnel. Aaron tried to lose them by driving down a cul-de-sac—the idea being that he'd bottleneck them and drive out on the sidewalk. But while two cars continued into the cul-de-sac to chase him, the others blocked the road and blocked the sidewalks by driving into driveways, putting the nose of their cars against cars parked in the driveways. As Aaron rounds out at the bottom and starts heading out on the sidewalk, up ahead is a wall of cars. Aaron tried to go around a car parked in a driveway, drove over some person's lawn to squeeze between the parked car and the garage, ran smack into a garbage can, slid out, and went down on the next lawn. I like to think he was laughing at this point.

"Aaron crawled over, turned off his bike, took off his helmet, and lay back on the ground with his hands stretched over his head. I think it's the only way he avoided the typical post-chase beating that's so often administered by police all pumped up on adrenaline. The report said that, once he was off the motorcycle, he offered no resistance.

"In California, you know, a police report will be written by one cop, and if other cops are involved, the reports they write are called supplements and are added to the main report. This police report was written by the first Highway Patrol officer, with numerous supplements for each cop involved in the chase. What was funny about the report was that the first cop went through each supplement and made up a list of each and every traffic violation he had witnessed or that was documented by any of the other police, making a single-spaced list of vehicle code violations that went on, and on, and on. After page after page of this (I believe more than a hundred violations were listed), it ended with him driving up on the sidewalk, which is apparently illegal. The sheer amount of work it must have taken that cop is impressive. Aaron laughed when I showed it to him.

"Aaron was charged with reckless driving (a misdemeanor) and evading (a misdemeanor) but not all of the violations listed in the report. In California, if you plead guilty to the charges listed on the complaint, the judge is free to sentence you as the judge sees fit, provided it is in the range of penalties provided for in the violations being admitted. And when we went to court, Aaron was given sixty days' home detention, over the DA's strong objections, by 'pleading the sheet.'

"I can't say Aaron was lucky, because of what happened later, but the day we went to court, the judge thought Aaron should rightfully do some county time but also had a policy of not wanting to sentence people to custody on his own birthday. And, on the one-out-of-three-hundred-and-sixty-five off-chance, it was: Aaron's court date had been set on the judge's birthday. In chambers, over birthday cake, the judge made the offer of home detention. The DA objected again and said that it was ridiculous for Aaron not to do at least thirty days; he'd originally wanted three months. I told Aaron what the deal was in the hallway, and he came into court to plead the sheet. The DA made a record regarding his objection to the sentence, and the judge sentenced Aaron to sixty days at home. Aaron was taken into custody for booking and processing, and was out a few hours later to set up the ankle monitor he wore for the next sixty days."

Paul smiled as he pictured it.

"I wish I could say it was good lawyering that got him that sentence, which is ridiculously good given what he did. But it wasn't. Just luck and a quirky old-time judge up in Martinez."

"Norton just *did* things," Jason Lockwood told me. "People who'd try to do the things he did would be trying to look cool, or tough, or this, or that. Norton just did them. That was the thing that made him so charming—he was so fucking happy to be doing exactly whatever it was he was doing. And you always knew that you could join him on that ride if you felt like it, and that it would be a fantastic ride."

I heard other stories, along the same lines. The Rats really did worship Aaron's memory; they wore T-shirts that had Aaron's photo on them, put stickers on their bikes that said: NORTON R.I.P. None of the Rats I'd met had had anything bad to say about him. He'd been promiscuous, they all agreed. But with the Rats, promiscuity was not a sin, and J.J. was the only person I talked to who made Norton Aaron sound creepy. "He banged hella girls," J.J. said. "He banged bar skanks behind his old lady's back. His *job* was to bang his own friends' old ladies. It was pretty fucked up, and he did a lot of it. He couldn't help himself."

It was hard to know what to believe, then or when J.J. told me that he'd had nothing at all to do with Norton's death—a denial that struck me as emphatic but oddly hedged.

"Norton had reasons to be looking over his shoulder," J.J. told me one night, over dinner at a Japanese restaurant in Berkeley. "Norton double-crossed a lot of people. He double-crossed me. But would I really want to *kill* him? If I really had messed with his girlfriend, and they had me dead to rights, why would I kill him? Why wouldn't I take my lumps and go away?"

The restaurant that we'd gone to was packed, and we were crowded against other couples. Some had stopped talking and started to eavesdrop.

"I don't know," I said.

"What I know," said J.J., "is that when he was riding home on his motorcycle, Norton was extremely depressed. He was emotionally compromised. He had been drinking. And if you think I could have killed him, not by shooting him, but by hitting him, without fucking up his bike or scratching my vehicle, or getting caught in any way, how good do you think I am?"

I didn't know what to tell him.

"Ask a combat veteran. Ask a special agent. Ask the guys who jump out of trees, upside down on parachute cords, in ninja suits. Ask them how they would kill that man. They wouldn't do it that way. *I* wouldn't do it that way. Just because I'm *capable* of doing it, that doesn't mean that I would."

Other Rats—Davey, Big Mike, and Trevor among them—had all told me crazy things: in Oakland, my crazy bar had become crazy high. Even so, this struck me as a poor line of defense, and a self-defeating one. Just then, I recalled something that Trevor had told me: "J.J. was always excitable," he'd said. "But he was more excitable when he got home from Iraq."

"What about Trevor?" I said.

"What about him?"

"Isn't there something that Trevor can do?"

"Trevor?" said J.J. "That captain's asleep! The captain's asleep and not leading his men! Members of his club are telling lies about me. But Trevor knows which side his bread's buttered on. He won't do a thing to stop it."

Had J.J. really buzzed the Rats out on the roads? I asked, and at first he said, "No."

Then J.J. backtracked.

"Some have tried to catch me," he said. "Some have tried to go outrun me, out on those twisty roads. But you know what? Sometimes I've caught *them*. I've waited behind them. I've passed them. I've passed them safely, because they weren't going that fast. They go slow! And they can't face the fact that their egos get hurt."

He seemed, to me, to be tangled in contradictions, caught up in his own wounded pride. Like the Rats, J.J. was in mourning. But the Rats were in mourning for Norton Aaron, while J.J. was mourning the loss of his club. After dinner I asked him, "How do you think things will end?"

"If they never said another thing bad about me," he said. "If they'd just let me go. . . . If it was like *Matrix* 3, that movie where the computers and people live together in harmony, not even acknowledging each other's existence—I would be perfectly happy with that. But the Rats have this burning in their gut. They know I'm a good guy. They want to shake my hand. They want to ride with me. But not on an officially approved Rat run. Because that would put me at an equal, eye-to-eye level with them. I'd outshine them. And they'd never be able to bang bar skanks behind their old ladies' backs again. Not while a guy like me was single."

I kept these things to myself. I didn't think there was more I would learn, or anything, short of the passage of time, that would defuse the conflict. But a few weeks later, in Concord—the town that Aaron had been trying to get to, according to the story that Paul, the lawyer, had told—I found myself talking with Aaron's brother, Davey.

"Jim had his headlights on a switch," Davey told me, as we sat at a table outside a strip-mall Starbucks. (It was the only time that I'd heard J.J. referred to as "Jim.") "He could turn them on and off and sneak up on people. And I think that Jim rode up beside Aaron, on his motorcycle, and elbowed him into the barrier. He's a skilled enough rider. It wouldn't leave any marks. And to me, that's the most likely scenario. But what do you do with that? Because for me, there's a reasonable doubt; it's possible that it's not him. And he's the kind of person that would try to capitalize on Aaron's death, use it to provoke fear and paranoia—to do what he did in the military in order to scare other people. He gains power by Aaron's death by acting crazy and making us think that he possibly did it. Either he did or he didn't, I don't like him either way. But one thing I remember him telling me was: never tell the same story twice to an interrogator. Tell a different story every time."

"What would you do," I asked, "if you did know for sure?"

"If I knew for sure? I think anybody would feel a responsibility to act. But if I was going to, it would have been in my best interest to act right away. Then it would be done and over with. Whatever time I would have served would have been done already. And no one else would be in harm's way or danger. So I considered it. And then I moved to Concord. I started taking classes, majoring in psychology, trying to understand my feelings, to gain perspective on the situation, and also to physically get away from him. What I didn't want was to be at some bar, drinking, and see him. I know how I'd feel at that moment. I don't like to see him. And so I came out here in order to not see him."

I was left wondering, not if the mystery surrounding Norton's death would ever be solved, but if it was in anyone's ultimate interest to solve it. If J.J. was guilty, he'd never admit it. If he was innocent, I didn't see how he'd prove it. It was a conundrum that he'd have to live with, and as for Davey, with his new life and young daughters—for him it made good sense to let things rest.

CHAPTER TEN

A few days after the Jews versus Gentiles fight night, Julio turned himself in to the Oakland police. Paul, the lawyer, predicted a prison sentence of four or five years. But Julio got lucky (sympathetic judge; overcrowded prisons) and ended up with a few months in county. He was lucky, too, to be out of the world for a while. John Firpo and I drove down for visiting hours at the Santa Rita Jail in Dublin to see him, and a thinner, healthier man met us on the other side of the glass. Julio had been keeping to himself, he told us, and reading: *Zen and the Art of Motorcycle Maintenance*, 7 *Habits of Highly Effective People*, *The Art of Seduction*. "Send more self-help books," he said when we asked what to get him.

Trevor, in the meanwhile, had lost the momentum he'd built up for Jews versus Gentiles. He drank even more now, and couldn't make sense of his love life. One night, at the Ruby Room, he pointed a tiny, tipsy Hispanic woman out to me.

"That's Dava," he said. "She roofied herself. Don't ask me

how. And on her way home, she stole someone's puppy. Don't ask me about that, either."

I didn't ask. Trevor did not elaborate. But Dava showed up at the clubhouse that weekend, when the Rats gathered to celebrate Trevor's thirty-ninth birthday. As was his custom, Trevor drank his age in beers. He was stumble-drunk by early evening, when Lucy and I arrived, and blind drunk by the time the sun had gone down. Shortly afterward, he picked up a samurai sword, put on a superfluous blindfold, and hacked away at a birthday piñata someone had strung up in back of the clubhouse. "Awesome," he said as the papier-mâché broke and a pile of raw meat—cheap steaks and sausages—fell out onto the gravel. A half hour later, Lucy and I walked over to say our good-byes. Dava was slumped on the bar and Trevor was glazed over, mystified, next to her.

"Trevor?" I said.

He looked up and slurred.

"Piggy . . ."

I was taken aback: Piggy, of course, is the kid who gets slaughtered, sacrificially, in William Golding's *Lord of the Flies*. But I understood Trevor's meaning: it was the first time, since we were both kids, that he had threatened me with violence; the closest I'd come to catching a glimpse of my childhood bully.

"Don't ever call me that again," I told him. But Trevor was too drunk to talk about it then, or remember much about it afterward. Later, I asked about the novel, which, Trevor told me, the Rats had all read. "That book meant a lot to us," he said, and the Rats all agreed that Trevor was right—the novel really had spoken to them.

"We were all lost boys, before finding the club," Timmers told me.

"Ask Trevor about the pig's head," another Rat said.

"The pig's head?"

"The pig's head we put on a stake, up in front of the club-house."

When I did ask him, Trevor grinned, slightly.

"Which time?" he said.

Later that week, Trevor took me on what he called a reconnaissance mission, down to the Victory Warehouse, a few blocks away on San Pablo Avenue.

West Oakland was full of buildings like the Victory. Many were abandoned. Others had been converted, with or without the necessary permits, into squats, marijuana grows, or semi-legitimate live/work spaces. This one had once been a part of the Victory Stables; an old sign still advertised: LIVERY SERVICE ★ GROOMING *15¢.*

Now the warehouse served as a rehearsal space for EinStye, a thrash metal band whose members lived in the building's back rooms and hosted parties and barbecues in its fenced-off front yard. These parties were smaller than ones the Rats threw. But the Victory drew a different crowd, and Trevor, still on the lookout for fight night prospects, made a point of attending. Tonight, he said, we were going to something called Hoodslam.

It was a Friday, and West Oakland's recyclers were out in force, jamming San Pablo up with their shopping carts, blocking large swaths of the sidewalk. All of them asked us for change as we parked, checked to make sure that we'd locked the car doors, and walked over to the warehouse. I looked for the recycler the Rats had beaten up on fight night. Trevor ignored the shopping cart people entirely.

"A few nights ago, I woke up," he told me. "A crackhead was pissing on the clubhouse door. Not in the gutter in front of the clubhouse. Not in the driveway next door. Right on my front door. I could smell the piss. And I'd heard him. So I grabbed my shotgun and picked up a shovel.

"The crackhead's still there when I open the door. Dick in hand, shaking the piss off. I whacked him with the shovel. I'd broken his arm, I could tell—it went limp immediately. Actually, I think I did the guy a favor: you could see the life jump right back into his eyes. But then I walked back inside and turned on the Xbox—I'd been playing Star Wars Battlefront— and got the highest score I've ever gotten. Isn't that something? My front door still smells like piss, though."

The warehouse was surrounded by a chain-link fence, which Trevor now rattled. The man who opened it took six bucks from me and waved Trevor in, gratis.

Inside, the lighting was dim; the walls were temporary, made out of plywood; there were no windows. A wrestling ring took up a third of the room and Trevor looked it over, approvingly—it was much newer than the Rats' own. "These ropes are tighter than ours," he said. "The floor's bouncier, too. There's a metal spring in the middle. A boxing ring is really just a stage with ropes—it has some give, but hit your head and you'll get a concussion. Wrestling is a whole other science."

The members of EinStye, set up in a corner, were running through a series of lightning-fast instrumentals. Some sounded familiar, in ways that I couldn't quite place. Others did not sound like music at all. Trevor waited for the band to finish and walked up to say hello.

By this point, Rats were introducing me to their friends as a writer who had "embedded" with them. It wasn't something that I'd ever say: the Rats were not soldiers (although many of them had been soldiers), and Oakland was not quite a combat zone. But then, the Rats never were all too clear on what I was doing around them, or why. Some thought I was writing a book—which I really was doing by now. Others seemed simply to enjoy the fact that they were important enough to embed with. But at the Victory, Trevor introduced me, much more accurately, as a new guy in Oakland.

EinStye's drummer jumped up from his stool and stuck out his hand to greet me. By and large, people in Oakland were friendly; all the more so when I found myself in the Rats' company. But the drummer—a skinny white kid in a basketball jersey—was especially nice.

"Oakland's amazing," he told me. "A beautiful, terrible, crazy, amazing place."

Through a doorway that separated the Victory's main space from its kitchen area, I saw a bathroom, and a back room with couches, armchairs, and a dressing rack. There were cases of beer on the floor in that room, and the couches were piled high with bric-a-brac: plastic lobsters; Mexican wrestling masks; a stuffed pony that looked like a rocking horse without its rockers; a bucket full of carpenter's tools—drills and staple guns. While I was looking, two men brushed past us and sat down in the armchairs. They had thick beards and thick arms, and must have weighed close to three hundred pounds each. Aside from their tattoos, they looked exactly alike and equally unfriendly. They did not acknowledge us at all, and Trevor and I stayed out of their way.

"Not your people?" I said.

"I don't know them."

"Not your circus?"

"Not my monkeys. But I do know that two guys put this tournament on—which is impressive because the production values are so much higher than what you'd expect from a two-man team. I don't think these guys are those guys. But those guys are the guys that I'd like to meet."

He unzipped his backpack, took out two cans of Bud Light, and handed me one. A flyer on the wall announced a starting time of 8:00 p.m., and at 6:56 now, not much was happening.

We finished our beers, and two more that Trevor fished out from his backpack. Eventually, the audience filtered in.

This crowd was younger than crowds I'd seen at the clubhouse, made up of kids in their teens or early twenties—punks and potheads, clerks from the Emeryville Apple Store, hipsters with fixie bikes—along with a few kids who couldn't have been much older than ten or twelve. They stood around drinking, smoking blunts and cigarettes. Everyone seemed to know everyone else. A few people recognized Trevor and, someone told him, he had been wrong: Hoodslam had just one promoter. Sam Khandaghabadi was a wrestler himself. When we met him, we found him to be remarkably polite, in the way that the children of immigrants sometimes are. Sam's parents had emigrated from Iran, in 1983. His father, Mahmoud, was a civil engineer. Sam had lost his mother, Soudabeh, to cancer when he was still in grade school. Wrestling, which had been a minor obsession, became a major escape. Sam took his first wrestling lessons at the age of fourteen and had his first match just after his sixteenth birthday. He was twenty-five now, working three days a week at a T-shirt company and wrestling, on the independent circuit, as Sheik Khan Abadi—or, sometimes, as the Dark Sheik—though he looked more like a pirate, or a Persian prince, with black hair that curled down to his shoulders, delicate features, a slim, athletic physique. He was wearing a T-shirt that read:

HOODSLAM
THIS IS REAL

Sam had been up for most of the week, he told us, working out the evening's details. Still, there was time for a beer and, in Sam's case, a couple of bong hits, followed by a joint a few of the wrestlers were passing around. Ten or twelve of them had arrived already and begun to change into the costumes dictated by story lines Sam had sketched out for them: Ninja versus Mafia Don; Zombie versus Circus Clown; Chupacabra versus Man in a Prawn Suit. The man in the prawn suit looked like something you'd see in front of a fast-food fish restaurant. But the chupacabra wore fangs, face paint, and creature-feature contact lenses that turned his pupils into wide, vertical slits—he was beautifully made up—and the ninja could have been a body double for Bruce Lee. Sam gave them high fives, cleared a space on the couch, sat down, and pulled a bagful of weed out of his pocket.

"Smoke?" he asked.

I said yes, and found that Sam's stuff was dispensary-grade, stronger than anything I'd tried before. Trevor refused, politely, and wandered away. Then Sam said, "Sit," and I sat and smoked with him, passing the bong back and forth. Listening, I lost track of time.

"This is our release," Sam was saying. "The only time we can all wrestle high." Then he stood up and I stood up, too, steadied myself, and followed him out to the yard. A group of men had gathered on the sidewalk in front of San Pablo Liquor Store, on the other side of the avenue, but they weren't paying attention to us. There were two SROs on that block, and an anarchist collective called the Holdout. A police car drove past the buildings and slowed down, slightly. The minutes turned into aquarium minutes. Sam took a pack of Marlboros out, lit one, and started talking.

"Oakland is the melting pot," he said. "It's like Jerusalem. Jerusalem, before the Crusades. The dark side of that is a whole lot that's negative. It's easy to fall into drugs here. There's violence. There's hookers, crackheads, and thugs—all up on this block. Did you know that someone got shot—right there, in front of the liquor store?"

Sam pointed across the street.

"Shot in the head, but the guy didn't die. He actually got up afterward. Didn't even lose consciousness. . . ."

It occurred to me that Sam must have been stoned all the time; there was no other way to explain his ability to form complete sentences when I could barely form words. Then I heard a crash, and the sound of something getting dragged across the floor inside the warehouse. Sam turned around toward the entrance, continued his thought.

"You can't always count on that happening," he said, and put his Marlboro out.

Back in the warehouse, Sam pulled a stack of index cards out of his pocket, gathered the wrestlers, and ran them through the night's set list. People in masks or more elaborate getups were milling all around us. I counted twenty-four wrestlers, and a few other people besides. One man wore a referee's jersey over a Winnie-the-Pooh costume. Another was picking burrs out of the bottom half of a Pink Panther suit. A ring announcer ran into the room, changed out of his street clothes and into a tux with tails. He was tall and formal, crane-like, with pomaded hair. The tuxedo fit him perfectly. He nodded to the drummer, who hit the snare and started a slow-burning drumroll. Sam ran around the room checking last-minute details, the chupacabra straightened his fangs, and then the announcer walked out through the crowd, turned on a micro-phone, and climbed through the ropes.

"Ladies and gentlemen," he said, in a shatterproof voice, but the crowd had already gone crazy. People around me were screaming, beside themselves with joy and anticipation. And, it turned out, Hoodslam's production values were extremely high. Wrestlers back-flipped off of the top ropes, tossed chairs at each other, threw themselves out of the ring, onto the con-crete floor, into the audience. EinStye played loud and fast, and the ring announcer drank from the bottles offered to him and puffed on countless blunts without losing his composure. Some of the bouts resolved themselves in a matter of seconds. Others formed a feedback loop with the audience and went on for ten minutes or more. During the intermission, a man and a woman in black leather gear brought the bucket I'd seen earlier into the ring. They put cigarettes out on each other's arms, stapled playing cards to their tongues and foreheads, broke lightbulbs off inside of their mouths. The crowd went apeshit: there was blood, lots of it, and the staple gun sounded like a starter pistol. It was hard to watch, phantasmagorical, and hard to look away from. But when the lights dimmed I saw Trevor's face, lit from below by the glow of his iPhone. He was standing a few yards away from me, frowning, texting or tapping out notes, oblivious to everything that was going on around him.

Sam wrestled once when the wrestling resumed. He'd changed during the intermission and was shirtless now, in purple parachute pants, gold-colored shoes, and dark makeup that all but obscured his features, and he was lightning-quick inside the ring, performing diving Hurricanranas, flying drop kicks, Tilt-A-Whirl headscissors, and his "coolest-sounding, least impressive move"—an inverted atomic drop—all in the space of a minute or two. Afterward, he stood by the dressing-room door, stage-directing, glancing down at his index cards, answering the questions I'd finally managed to formulate.

"All of us are professional wrestlers," he said. "Some I met a few months ago. Others I've known for years. Tomorrow night we'll be back on the circuit, working high school gyms, playing totally different characters. None of us will be drunk or stoned. We'll do it for nothing or next to nothing. We'll drive hundreds of miles for the shittiest payoffs, and when we perform, we'll get told what to do. I'll leave town on a Thursday, wrestle Friday, Saturday, and Sunday, come back to Oakland on Monday, work for three days in a row, and do it all over again. I'll wrestle in Vegas one day, drive down to L.A. the next, and end up in Reno, or Oregon. That's ten, twelve hours straight in the car—your neck, your back, the road food you're eating—all of that's worse for your body, almost, than wrestling. We'll do cities, small towns. I'll do Fresno, Martinez, and Hayward. Sacramento's a wrestling town. The smaller towns are especially good. Faraway towns. There's nothing to do there till we come around. The further out you go, the crazier the crowds get."

Most of the wrestlers had day jobs, Sam told me. The chupacabra had moved up to Reno for warehouse work, which he'd been laid off from a few months earlier—a loss that was good for his wrestling but tough on his wife and his children. The mean-looking twins, who tag-teamed as Rick Scott and Scott Rick Stoner, were counselors at a school for troubled children. The mafia don delivered pizzas. I never found out what the referee in the Winnie-the-Pooh costume did for a living, but the ring announcer, who really was a professional ring announcer, smoked dope in his off time and did maintenance work on the side, and Matthew, the man in the Pink Panther suit, worked the door at the Hotsy Totsy Club, a bar on San Pablo Avenue in Albany. I ran into him there a few weeks later and the two of us had a long conversation about the decade he'd spent as a meth addict. Matthew was in his midtwenties, blond and lanky, a California boy from the Central Valley, on the other side of the Oakland Hills. He'd left the state only once, to spend a few weeks with a female friend, also a methamphetamine addict, who'd moved out to North Carolina. That relationship had burned itself out. But Matthew was home now and clean, or close to it, and on my way out of the bar I asked him what he could see himself doing in five years, or ten years, or twenty. "Well," Matthew said, in a way that made me wonder if the question had ever occurred to him. "What I'd like to do someday is referee, but without the Pink Panther suit."

At Hoodslam, Matthew had ended up on the dressing-room floor, struggling not to throw up inside the Pink Panther's head. Winnie-the-Pooh had passed out in an armchair—heat exhaustion, pot, and booze had done both of the referees in—and now, with the referees gone, all of the wrestlers piled into the ring. They boasted and drank, passed joints around, and screamed at the crowd that was screaming at them. The night dissolved in a THC haze while Sam hung back by the dressing-room entrance and watched.

When the lights came up Trevor was gone. When I looked at my phone, I saw that he'd texted. Dava had been mugged, in front of a bus stop on Telegraph Avenue. Her friend, Pilar, had been hit in the head with a bottle.

"Crackhead," Trevor had texted.

"Gonna get him," he'd said.

It was close to midnight, and Lucy was spending the week in New York. I sent Trevor another text, which he never replied to; it would be a few days before I saw him again. I didn't know how I was going to get home. In the end, I asked Sam for a lift.

He drove his old Honda Accord, carefully, in the right-hand lane. We passed shopping-cart people, a couple of corner boys, a streetwalker standing by herself in front of the California Hotel, a few blocks up from the Rats' clubhouse. Seeing her, I thought of Jim Saleda, a vice cop Trevor had introduced me to during my first trip out to Oakland. Jim had been a kid in the 1970s, when, just as Oakland was falling apart, the A's had won three World Series. But he knew enough of the history to tell me that during those years, this stretch of San Pablo had been the Bay Area's main track for prostitutes. Huey Newton ran girls out of his Ghost Town club, next door to the barbershop that had become the East Bay Rats' clubhouse, and the city's pimps had hosted Players Balls, annually, at the Zanzibar, one of three nightclubs down the street, inside the California Hotel. Back then, the California Hotel had been the fanciest place on San Pablo. James Brown, Billie Holiday, Mahalia Jackson, and Ray Charles had all played there and Sly and the Family Stone had been regulars. Now, the California was an SRO—a freeway overpass had been put through, within spitting distance of its second story—and Saleda's team did most of its work in East Oakland. "Today," he had told me, "the West Oakland hookers don't even have pimps."

Sam talked as he drove, about Hoodslam, the characters he'd created, their genealogies and backstories, flaws and aspirations. The matches I'd just seen involved long-standing rivalries, he said, which most Hoodslam fans would have been clued into. The ring announcer's stage patter had been thick with local references, inside jokes, and callbacks. Most of the instrumentals EinStye played had sounded familiar, too, because they were blitzkrieg renditions of television-show sound tracks or theme songs to outdated video games. Hoodslam had been packed with referential bits that I'd missed out on or been too old, stoned, or uninformed to understand. But for most people in the audience, the night's chemically induced dislocations would have been accompanied by a very real sense of déjà vu—in some cases, for a time that they were far too young to have experienced directly.

"It's like a comic book, or a movie," Sam told me. "Something you can disappear, or lose yourself in. The eighties references help—all of that stuff we absorbed in the womb. The more we throw at you, the more immersive Hoodslam becomes. Although, of course, all of us are immersed in it already. Wrestling is our life. And most of us live in Oakland. But there's no wrestling *in* Oakland. That's what Hoodslam is really about."

He popped the ashtray open, took a pack of cigarettes out, and shook a funnel-shaped joint up out of the pack.

"The people I saw smoking dope in the ring, was it really dope they were smoking?"

"As far as I know, I'd say yes. You'd have to ask people personally. But in my experience, yes."

"And you're high every time you do it?"

"I'm high every time I write the show. I'm high when I go out with flyers. I'm high at all the promotions we do. Everything I do for the show I do high. The truth is that I'm constantly in some sort of pain. I need to self-medicate. And pills just knock me out."

Sam told me that he had a rib that was cracked or bruised permanently—he didn't have medical insurance and couldn't afford to do anything about it. He'd torn a knee ligament a few years back (that still bothered him, too) and hurt his neck, wrists, and ankles on several occasions. When I asked about the matches themselves, whether or not they were scripted, he told me that conditions varied. "Sometimes it'll be, 'Duck this, trip over that, roll here, and flip that,'" he said. "Other times, we'll just go. Really fight. You open it up for me, I'll open it up for you. There'll be some real shots in there. You're going to take some punishment."

"And when you land outside the ring? You know how to roll. You train for it. You aren't masochists, right?"

"I wouldn't say that," said Sam. "If you roll, you lose the sound. And it's all about that 'smack!' When you hit the concrete, you want to go 'thud!' You want to go 'splat!' It's a sickness in wrestling: you want the applause from the crowd. You want to hear that 'pop!' And we put the pop ahead of our bodies. If we didn't, we wouldn't be wrestling."

CHAPTER ELEVEN

Dava's friend Pilar ended up in the hospital, her scalp full of surgical staples. Trevor spent the next few days looking for her assailant, riding all over town, hassling street people, barflies, low-level criminals. No one he'd talked to would give the man up.

"I really did think that I'd find him," he said the next time I saw him. We were at Mama Buzz, a café close to the clubhouse that was a regular pit stop on Trevor's afternoon circuits. Trevor's friend Billy was working the counter. "I was going to break the guy's legs," Trevor said.

Billy said, "Well, we can take care of the bus stop."

Billy lived a few blocks up the avenue, in an apartment that looked down directly on the bus stop where Dava and Pilar had been mugged. He knew for a fact that drug dealers sold heroin out from under the bus stop's glass awning and thought that they also sold speed, and he'd grown used to boozehounds and addicts who shuffled back and forth between the two shops that bookended the stop—Saigon Market, which sold beer and lottery tickets but not liquor, and the Telegraph Quality Market, which sold liquor and cigarettes but not lottery tickets. He'd see them pissing on the bus stop bench, puking, or passing out on it. Every so often he'd witnessed a mugging, a fistfight, or something worse. He'd called the police several times, but the bus stop fell under AC Transit's jurisdiction—there was nothing the police would do—and AC Transit would always give him the runaround.

"The cops don't like that bus stop themselves," Billy said. "The last time I called them, they told me flat-out, 'Why don't you just drive a car into it?'"

Trevor leaned over the counter and lowered his voice. "We could do that," he said. "We could get a truck, go for total destruction. Or, we could try area denial."

"Put honey, or tar, on the bench," said Billy.

"Roofing tar would be good."

"Put tar on the bench and tacks in the roofing tar."

"Spray bear spray all over the bus stop."

"What's bear spray?" I asked.

"Bear spray would stink up the block."

"Get six guys with sledgehammers, smash it to shit."

"Weld bars to the outside. Make people crawl to hang out in there."

"Ten guys with sledgehammers."

"Smash it to shit."

"Or steal it. Load the thing onto a flatbed. Dump it off of the Berkeley pier."

In the end, Trevor decided to lift the bus stop off its foundation, smash it, and leave it out in the street.

"I like it," said Billy. "It's simple."

"It'll be out there for months," Trevor said.

That night, when the Ruby Room closed, Trevor met Billy and four other friends at the bus stop. The next day, he texted me. "All good," he wrote. But when I drove down to meet him at Mama Buzz, I passed the markets and saw a new bus stop, standing right where the old one had been.

Trevor and Billy were out on the sidewalk outside the café. Billy had a cigarette going. Trevor was holding a mugful of coffee.

"We didn't count on Clear Channel," he said.

Trevor and Billy hadn't realized that Clear Channel had made a deal with the city. The company sold ads on the bus stops in Oakland and contracted for their repair.

"Little Clear Channel elves were here at six in the morning," said Billy. "By seven, it was as if nothing had happened."

Trevor sipped from his mug and screwed up his features.

"Elves should take over the whole fucking city," he said.

That evening, Trevor called and asked if I'd drive him home from the Ruby Room. I assumed he was drunk and was surprised, when I got to the bar, to find him more or less sober. At the clubhouse, he asked me to wait and came out holding an object that I couldn't see. He asked me to pop the trunk, got back in the passenger seat and then we drove to a dark block that I'd never stopped on before. In the trunk, I saw a single-bit ax—a big one. Trevor grabbed it by the head and held it so that the handle ran down the length of his leg.

"Come on," he said and started to walk, not too quickly, toward Telegraph Avenue. It was very late now. The only person we saw was Billy, waiting for us on his corner. Trevor shook his hand and threw out a couple of names.

"Texted them all," Billy said. "All of them said that they'd be here."

"We'll wait," said Trevor.

We stood by the bus stop, watching the traffic lights turn. There was a sign advertising Subway sandwiches, and a route map, framed behind glass, mounted at eye level behind the bench. I never used AC Transit—I'd barely been on BART—but, I saw now, the map was beautiful. The routes, traced in blue and purple, looked like veins running all through the city, and the city itself looked like it had been rolled, like a carpet, down from the hills to the water. I'd begun tracing one route with my finger when I heard Trevor say, "Fuck it."

Glass shattered and fell all around me. I threw my arms up over my head.

"You didn't wait very long for your friends!"

Trevor looked at me for a moment, shook his head, and turned his attention back to the bus stop. Whatever he'd hoped to do to the mugger he did to it—calmly, methodically—walls, bench, and ceiling. The map's frame fell to the sidewalk and broke. I should have known that this was where things were headed; I'd seen the ax, after all. Still, I felt indignant.

"You could have told me," I said when Trevor was done.

"Would you have come?"

I considered the question. It seemed insane to just bust up the bus stop. Then again, the police themselves had suggested it, Trevor's friend had gotten hurt there—maybe it was insane not to.

"Of course," I said.

CHAPTER TWELVE

The cops never came. Clear Channel gave up on the bus stop. But Trevor decided that he would lie low, just in case, and I spent my time driving around Oakland, or at the library—Oakland's main branch, across the street from the Ruby Room. I'd found an archive, on the second floor, that contained a treasure trove of photographs, oral histories, labor histories, maps and postcards, catalogs, dissertations, and old phone directories. The file cabinets were crammed with pamphlets, communiqués, and ancient newspaper clippings:

- Police Officer Makes Pipe Cleaner Animals as Hobby
- Gin-Selling Negress Borrows Baby to Soften Judge's Heart
- San Pablo Avenue Declared to Be Most Disgraceful Thoroughfare in Oakland

I made photocopies, filled notebooks with facts. At night, I drove around, meeting people and collecting stories. At home, I'd try to put my notes in some sort of order:

Luis María Peralta, the old land grant holder: His eldest son, Ignacio (1791–1874), was an Indian fighter. His second son, José Domingo (1795–1865), became a justice of the peace. The third, Antonio María (1801–1879), was a bon vivant, fond of wrestling, rodeos, and bullfights. The youngest son, Vicente (1812–1871), was tall, fair, and bearded, but toward the end of his life he'd become paralyzed and blind.

•

Che Guevara was Don Luis's great-great-great-grandson.

•

Oakland's first mayor, Horace Carpentier, became the largest landowner in California. In the 1860s, Carpentier transferred control of the waterfront to the Central Pacific Railroad—which turned Oakland into the terminus of America's first transcontinental railroad. Then he returned to New York and died, in 1918, a millionaire several times over. At Columbia University, the Dean Lung Professorship of Chinese Studies continues to honor the memory of Carpentier's Chinese valet.

•

Disgusted by the theft of Oakland's waterfront, Carpentier's partner Andrew Moon quit California and spent the rest of his days on the Sandwich Islands.

•

The third partner, Edson Adams, remained in Oakland, married the city's first schoolteacher, and prospered, raising a son, also named Edson, who became a bank president and built the fanciest mansion in Piedmont—one with ten thousand square feet of living space, two solariums, an elevator that led to the master bedroom, and a family room designed by Julia Morgan, who went on to build Hearst's castle at San Simeon.

●

The first Oakland police officer to die in the line of duty was killed, by a squatter whom he had been sent to evict, in 1867.

●

In 1872, Oakland annexed Brooklyn, a town due east of the city. In 1909—three years after the San Francisco earthquake—Oakland annexed four other suburbs east of Lake Merritt, folding Mills, the exclusive women's college, and the neighborhoods around it into East Oakland. In 1916, a Chevrolet factory opened nine blocks away from Mills' campus. This was the first auto plant in the West, and in the years that followed Durant and Chrysler, Willys-Overland, Peterbilt, Caterpillar, and International Harvester all built car, truck, or tractor plants in or outside of the city. In the 1920s, civic leaders began to tempt fate, advertising Oakland as a "Detroit of the West."

●

During the Depression, hundreds of homeless men lived in unused sewer pipes owned by the American Concrete and Steel Pipe Company in Oakland. The men elected a mayor, a police chief, and a go-between to negotiate squatter's rights with the company. They called their camp "Miseryville," though the newspapers called it "Pipe City." The men pooled their money, lived on mulligan stew, and dispersed peacefully when their pipes had been sold.

·

In 1915, a former congressman named Joseph Knowland acquired an ownership stake in the *Oakland Tribune*. Hermina Peralta Dargie, who sold it to him, was a granddaughter of Luis María Peralta.

·

The mansion Joe Knowland bought for himself was the old Adams mansion, purchased directly from Edson Adams (the second) in 1945—the year that California's senior senator, Hiram Johnson, died in office. Earl Warren, who'd been protégé of Joe Knowland, appointed Knowland's son William to fill Johnson's vacant seat, and in 1953, William became majority leader of the United States Senate.

·

In a town where power had always been held by monopoly, collective actions—up to and including revolts—had become an only available means of political expression. But as California Republicans, the Knowlands opposed collective actions of *any* kind, and the Knowlands had a lock on the city. At the height of his powers, Joe Knowland ran Oakland's Community Chest, the Downtown Property Owners Association, local chapters of the Red Cross and March of Dimes, and the Oakland Chamber of Commerce. His son was the most powerful Republican politician in Washington, after the president. And, as the owner, publisher, editor, and president of the *Oakland Tribune*, Knowland controlled the fourth estate—which is to say, the means of reporting on all events in and around the city—as well as the city itself.

During World War II, Oakland's port and army base served as debarkation points for troops headed to the Pacific Theater; they were the last American places that thousands of soldiers, sailors, and marines would see.

•

At the same time, Oakland's Central Station became an arrival point for tens of thousands of workers, many of them African Americans who came to work in the local shipyards and settled near the station, in West Oakland. Overcrowding became a concern: during this period, the black population of West Oakland quintupled. But when blacks tried to move out into surrounding neighborhoods, they found their way blocked by restrictive housing covenants.

•

"The trouble," as it was described in an editorial in the *Oakland Observer*, "is that the Negro newcomer does not concede that the white man has the right to be alone with his kind. If the white man does not want the Negro sitting alongside him in the white man's restaurants, or does not want the association of the Negro anywhere else, this might be attributed to racial prejudice. Yet, in the final analysis, the white man has the right of racial prejudice if he so desires. If he does not care to associate with anyone, he is not compelled to do so."

•

An old real estate pamphlet, quoted in Beth Bagwell's *Oakland: The Story of a City*: "It is probably unnecessary even to mention that no one of African or Mongolian descent will ever be allowed to own a lot in Rockridge or even rent any house that may be built there."

•

Rockridge was the Oakland neighborhood that Lucy and I had settled in.

•

In 1947, the MacArthur Freeway split Oakland in half, along its long north-south axis, running between the hills, where the haves lived, and the flats, where Oakland's poor neighborhoods were, and cutting West Oakland off from the city's downtown. Two years later, West Oakland was designated as "blighted" and entire neighborhoods were razed.

•

In 1958, William Knowland returned to Oakland, ran for governor, and lost. After taking over the *Oakland Tribune*, he went on to play a leading role (as the heavy) in the start of the Free Speech Movement, then became head of California's Republican Party—a post he held from 1959 to 1967 (the year following Joe Knowland's death), when leadership passed to Ronald Reagan.

•

In 1974, the *Tribune* celebrated its hundredth birthday. Two days later, William Knowland—facing a second divorce and in Dutch with the mob in Las Vegas—blew his brains out by the Russian River. It was the first time since the city's founding that Oakland came out from under monopoly control, at which point it entered a long twilight of corruption, kickbacks, and civic shortsightedness, from which it has never really emerged.

In West Oakland, urban renewal had continued apace. In 1960, hundreds of West Oakland homes were demolished (in some cases, by Abdo S. Allen's Sherman tank) to make way for an enormous postal facility. A few years later, Bay Area Rapid Transit began to build a track directly above Seventh Street—the main dining, shopping, and entertainment district for black Oakland. All of the businesses along Seventh Street disappeared. A few blocks away, on Sixteenth Street, the city's Central Station was shut down, fenced off, and abandoned.

The city had other zombie buildings: Oakland's meeting ground, the Oakland Auditorium, which had closed a few years earlier; the Cathedral Building, a lovely historic flatiron on Latham Square; the Tribune Tower, which Joe Knowland had modeled after St. Mark's Campanile in Venice. But Central Station was the one I kept returning to, even if I could not get inside, or (thanks to the fences) even near it. This was fitting, poetic: the end of the railroads, turned into a terminus for other American dreams. But every once in a long while, one of Oakland's abandoned landmarks would flicker back to life. You'd drive past, see Central Station or the Tribune Tower lit up from inside. Then, having stopped to investigate, you'd find some movie being shot there: an HBO film about the Hemingways; a thriller starring Clint Eastwood. A day or two later, the lights would all be off again.

But, for all that, Oakland was still very beautiful, and not just up in the hills or in its pockets of affluence. In and around the Lower Bottoms, I'd stroll down streets that were stacked, wall to wall, with lovely Victorians—many of which dated back to the 1870s and still retained their original details and fixtures. This part of West Oakland was closer to San Francisco than anywhere else in the city; the very first stop on the BART line, it was eight minutes away from the Embarcadero. Despite the crime, and pollution from the adjacent port, the freeways, and the local Superfund site, it was the only place in Oakland that Lucy and I ever considered moving to.

"West Oakland really is beautiful," an Oakland cop told me. "One time, I had to kick a door down in West Oakland. It was a lovely mahogany door, a hundred years old, at least. I remember thinking, 'My God, I really want this door! And I've just broken it.'"

East Oakland, on the far side of the lake, seemed like a different city. Statistically, parts of it were as dangerous as, or more dangerous than, the very worst parts of West Oakland. But the flats of East Oakland were spread out, like parts of Los Angeles, featureless, grim. Outside of Mills College, with its tree-lined campus, gated now and fenced, and its buildings by Julia Morgan, East Oakland seemed to have no history at all.

One by one, the East Bay's shipyards and car, truck, and tractor plants had all closed. Chevrolet's assembly line had been the last one to go, in 1963. Where the car factory had been, car culture was all that remained. Cruising, flossing—guys with no place to be would drive up and down, hanging halfway out of their cars. Locally this was called "siding"—the police hated siding—but siding gave birth to the sideshows: impromptu car shows that doubled as movable dance parties. The sideshows started in the eighties; some said, the seventies. They involved hundreds or thousands of people who took over East Oakland's intersections, spun their cars around, or parked and danced on top of them. Complaints were lodged: for most of East Oakland's residents (especially the older ones), the sideshows were disruptive at best. But there wasn't too much that Oakland's cops could do to stop them. By the nineties, sideshows had gotten so big that even the cops came to view them with a sort of grudging respect.

"Typically, I worked Thursday, Friday, Saturday, and Sunday," Jason England told me. England was a big guy, no-nonsense, and tough—in the navy, he'd served as an interrogator at Guantánamo Bay. As an Oakland policeman, he'd worked all over the city. For several years, he'd spent his weekends busting up sideshows, or trying to.

"During the summer months," he said, "you'd deal with the sideshow on all of those nights. Four nights a week you just lived it. There were like ten of us on duty, and straight from the start to the end of our shifts, it was just sideshow. We'd drive around. You'd see a group of ten people and bust them about. Get them moving. Take someone to jail right off. If you could keep it from getting established, then you could handle it. But once you let fifty people, or more, get into one location, you basically had to call in the whole city. That could happen within fifteen minutes. Drive around a corner, all of the sudden there's ninety people there. Try to break that up, you'd have a full-fledged riot. One night, we had two thousand people outside of the Eastmont Mall—some promoter had oversold a rap concert. It got crazy that night. People were beating each other, shooting each other. All you could do was watch. The sky's filled with rocks and bottles, you're looking at it, and you're just kind of trying to maintain. But even on a regular night: one thousand people in the Eastmont Mall parking lot. They'd use their cars to block exits and entrances. There would be five to ten cars spinning doughnuts inside the crowd, hundreds of people dancing on top of parked cars. And as they were spinning, the drivers shot guns out their windows. That's what happened when sideshows reached critical mass. For quite a few years, we were actually doing a good job of keeping them small. Then Joe Samuels came in as the chief of police. One night, he came out himself. He tried to stop the crowd. They pelted him with bottles, so he switched our tactics to traffic control. We'd take ten of our guys, put 'em on traffic duty.

Keep people from getting into the mall. What happened then was the sideshow just formed in a circle around us. You'd take another ten guys, and another ten guys—soon you've got the entire police force trying to block off the mall while the sideshow goes on all around it. On patrol you'd hear the dispatcher say, 'There's a shooting in progress over on Ninety-eighth and MacArthur. There's a robbery in progress. There's a burglary in progress.' She'd list twenty calls, thirty calls. Serious, in-progress calls. Murders. Robberies. Car chases. 'Is there any officer in the city of Oakland that can respond to any one of these calls?' There'd be dead silence. Everyone was tied up at the sideshow. It was crazy. It was just insane."

Once in a while, in East Oakland, I'd see a sedan peel off at an intersection, or spin a doughnut or two. But I never did see much of a crowd. A few times, I drove down to the Eastmont Mall—the epicenter of sideshow activities, where Jason England had logged all those hours. This was the place where the sideshows had started, and as soon as I saw it I understood why. For an inner-city mall, Eastmont was enormous: a full-size, two-story indoor mall, with the biggest, emptiest parking lot I'd seen since the day that Trevor and J.J. had taken me out to the Berkeley track. It turned out that Eastmont was as large as it was because it had been built on the very same spot where East Oakland's Chevrolet factory had stood. But the odd thing about Eastmont, now, was that it wasn't a mall anymore. Only a few shops were still open. Eastmont had had its own movie theater, but it, too, had closed. A ghost of the mall was still there, but it had been turned into a social services hub, called the Eastmont Town Center. The place where thousands of people had worked had become a place to get welfare checks, Plan B, methadone, library books, and prenatal vitamins. Sideshows took place elsewhere now: OPD had opened a substation in what had been the mall's main department store. For all intents and purposes, the place Jason England had told me about was long gone.

Online, I ordered DVDs with names like *Boomer Town* ("Take a journey to East Oakland Streets") and *Hyphy Exposed* ("From the makers of the multi-platinum smash hit *Ghetto Fights*"); the best ones all had the word "Sydewayz" somewhere in the title, and all of them backed up England's descriptions. The parties had been massive, with hundreds of people, or thousands. The cars had been nicer than ones you'd see now: box Chevs and old, tricked-out Buicks. Drivers pulled out all the stops for the camera, or acted as if no one was watching at all, while self-styled "matadors" danced in between their cars. There had been rules to the proceedings; sometimes, these had been codified in rap songs. And then, there were no rules at all. Once, an on-duty AC Transit bus had done the gas-break-dip in broad daylight while moving through a cheering crowd. But with no fixed place left for the sideshows to take over, the long-standing turf wars with OPD had shifted and changed, becoming guerrilla and hard to nail down. I never did see a sideshow. But at the same time, I was aware of other turf wars that were closer to home. One morning J.J. texted and told me that Rats had jumped him—tried to beat him up, right around the corner from me, in front of Cole Coffee.

I wrote back to tell him I'd meet him in person, then texted Trevor.

"What happened this morning?" I wrote.

"Big Mike," he wrote back. "It's that tattoo again."

CHAPTER THIRTEEN

In New York I'd met a man with a tattoo, not of Will Ferrell, but of the character Will Ferrell played in *Anchorman: The Legend of Ron Burgundy*. Can you imagine, walking around for the rest of your life with Ron Burgundy's face peeking up above your sock line? I imagined it often during my time with the Rats, who had more tattoos than I could count or keep track of.

Some of the tattoos were jokey, or frivolous. The club's treasurer, J.T., had a mustache tattooed on his knuckles and a monocle inked on his palm. Zhiva, who managed a bar, had a tattoo that read W.W.T.D.?—short for "What Would Travis Do?"—and Travis, who ran his own contracting business, had a tattoo that read I ♥ ZHIVA. Davey Fuller had Buddy Holly's face tattooed on his arm, not because he was especially fond of the singer's music but because the day he'd walked into the parlor happened to be the anniversary of Holly's death. But on Davey's other arm, a marine in World War I drag drove his bayonet into the body of a German soldier. It was a terrible image, like something out of Remarque, or Goya's *Disasters of War*. But Davey told me that he'd been inspired by a painting he'd seen at Camp David, during his own stint in the Marine Corps. "I've got some German ancestry," he said. "I don't separate one human being from another human being. We're all the same person. So to me, the image of one man driving his bayonet into another man's body is a way of depicting the tragedy of our shared human experience."

There were tattoos that the Rats had in common—ones that spoke to their shared history, and had obvious meanings—and others that took me some time to decode. It took months to find out that NOS VINCIMUS, a phrase Trevor and Norton Aaron had had tattooed across their collarbones, marked the memory of one perfect night at Ruby Room. That evening had kicked off with a backstreet fuck, in the alley behind the bar, then moved on to a fistfight out front. "We won," Trevor told me, "but then the cops chased us. We got away on our bikes—that was like winning again. We felt invincible, which is what those words mean in Latin." J.T. hadn't been at the Ruby that night, but he'd gotten the same tattoo, higher up on his neck. Later on, the phrase became a club catchphrase, along the lines of *Safety First!* or *What Could Possibly Go Wrong?*—a question best answered by other tattoos the Rats had.

To honor Big Nate's memory, Trevor had had a Jameson logo inked on his right arm. (Jameson was the whiskey that Nate had been drinking on the night of his death.) On their upper backs, Aaron, Davey, and Amariah Fuller had gotten the words שומר אחי —"my brother's keeper"—tattooed, in Hebrew. When Aaron died, other Rats had had the words inked on their backs, with ink that was mixed in with Aaron's ashes. Because Trevor's rat skull tattoo took up his whole back already, he'd gotten NORTON inked across his stomach.

But the tattoos that I saw most often were rat skulls, which the Rats had on their arms, their elbows, their chests, and their necks. Like John Firpo, Travis had a rat skull tattooed on the back of his own skull. Trevor had his enormous back tattoo, which had taken three sessions, and fifteen hours, to complete. And, I had heard, the skull on J.J.'s back had been even bigger.

The rat skull tattoos were vaguely threatening, like prison tattoos, and, of course, they were supposed to be permanent. Trevor told me that members who'd left the club amicably could keep their skulls, conditionally, after adding their entry and exit dates. Other Rats told me that J.J., who'd left on bad terms, never had gotten rid of his rat skull—it had become one more point of contention.

I could not imagine what the Rats would have done if a stranger had shown up at the bar sporting a rat skull like theirs. I asked Trevor once: "Would you talk to the guy or just beat him up automatically?" But it was the same with all either-or questions: Trevor would always agree, with a "Yep."

I had never seen J.J.'s rat skull tattoo. But during our dinner in Berkeley, I'd asked him about a tattoo on his bicep. It was of a motorcycle, a sixties-era track bike, he told me, with a #1 license plate that symbolized J.J.'s identification with the 1%, outlaw biker lifestyle.

J.J. had a daughter, a day job; he'd driven a minivan to the restaurant.

"Outlaw?" I'd wondered.

"Do you understand what I mean by the term?"

"I think so," I said.

"I mean that the laws of my moral code supersede the laws of the United States government. That they supersede the laws of the state of California. That I live my life outside the law and that I am okay with that fact."

I thought of Trevor, who was not an outlaw or a 1%-er. Now that J.J. was out of the club, none of the Rats were. But on his other arm, Trevor had a tattoo that rhymed with J.J.'s and spoke to a history all bikers shared. It was of a man, sitting on top of an old Harley-Davidson, holding beer bottles in both of his hands, with other beer bottles scattered on the ground all around him. The scene had been rendered in loving detail—copied, line for line, from a photo that Trevor had brought to the tattoo parlor.

Trevor knew most of what there was to know about the photo. He knew that it had been taken during a motorcycle rally, or riot, in Hollister, California, in the summer of 1947. He knew that the photo had run in *Life* magazine. And he knew that, in all likelihood, the shot had been faked: that the photographer had arranged the bottles just so, grabbed some inebriated stranger, and put him on top of another man's bike. But, Trevor said, the thought that the photo might have been staged didn't make much of a difference. "That picture put everything into one moment," he told me. "Even though it was posed, even if it wasn't his bike, and they put those beer bottles around the bottom. Whatever the story was. It captured something that all bikers yearn for. It's a classic bike, a classic look. But the man's slouch, how comfortable he is in the middle of chaos? That's something we all aspire to."

In *Life* (the issue dated July 21, 1947), the photo in question had taken up most of a page. The caption below it read: "CYCLIST'S HOLIDAY: He and friends terrorize a town," and the short accompanying story described motorcyclists rampaging through Hollister a few weeks earlier: "Racing their motorcycles down the main street and through traffic lights, they rammed into restaurants and bars, breaking furniture and mirrors. Some rested a while by the curb. Others hardly paused. Police arrested many for drunkenness and indecent exposure but could not restore order. Finally, after two days, the cyclists left with a brazen explanation. 'We like to show off. It's just a lot of fun.' But Hollister's police chief took a different view. Wailed he, 'it's just one hell of a mess.'" But *Life* was famous for its photographs—twenty million Americans saw its pictures every week—and in this case, the photo did much more work than the story itself.

The man on top of the Harley was overweight, with glassy, unfocused eyes. His belly spilled out from an unbuttoned shirt while, behind him, a skinny young man stood, hands in his pockets, gazing soberly into the lens. In the background, the letters on a storefront awning spelled: HOLLISTER.

Even motorcyclists who'd never been to Hollister sensed, right away, that the image was off. In a letter to *Life*'s editors, Paul Brokaw—who was himself the editor of *Motorcyclist* magazine—called it "very obviously arranged, and posed by an enterprising and unscrupulous photographer." Brokaw acknowledged that some sort of "disorder" had taken place in Hollister, but blamed "not the acts of 4,000 motorcyclists, but rather of a small percentage of that number, aided by a much larger group of non-motorcycling hell-raisers and mercenary-minded barkeepers." In what could have been seen as a tacit admission of guilt, *Life*'s editors printed Brokaw's letter without a response.

Of course, standards were different in 1947; back then, photos were faked as a matter of course, or simple convenience. ("We were always setting up pictures of some sort," a staff photographer for *Life* explained, many years later. "I felt that my job was to get the pictures. . . . We shot a gazelle and put it in a tree and waited for a cat to come. I didn't feel bad about it at all. It sounds terrible now, I know, and maybe my attitude would be different now. But it wasn't then, and I don't know what else to say about it. I know, I've been criticized a lot. But to me, I had to do what I did.") And yet, before the Hollister photograph's publication, motorcycling was seen, simply, as a sport and a leisure activity: a pursuit so clean-cut that movie stars like Clark Gable and Barbara Stanwyck appeared, in PR stills, on the backs of their bikes. The word "outlaw" existed, already, inside the motorcycling community, but was used, primarily, to refer to races that hadn't been sanctioned by the sport's governing body, the American Motorcyclist Association. Motorcycle clubs also existed, but club members wore sweaters instead of leathers (clubs that formed before World War II are still known as "sweater clubs"), and tended to be more demure. *Life*'s photograph changed all of that: along with Brokaw's letter and other, official pronouncements on behalf of motorcycling authorities, it caused a small percentage of motorcyclists to call themselves outlaws—by which they now meant something akin to "outcasts."

In that sense, the photograph didn't articulate the 1%, outlaw aesthetic so much as bring that aesthetic into being. But if their origin story was fictional, what did that say about the realities of modern-day bikers' lives? Trevor may not have cared, but if the fantasy had a foundation, I wanted to know what it was. After all, cats and gazelles did exist. And, I knew, *something* had happened at Hollister. Whatever it was held a key to Trevor's world—or, at least, the world as Trevor saw it.

The identity of the man on the Harley has never been firmly established. But in the late 1990s, as Hollister geared up to celebrate the rally's fiftieth anniversary, the skinny young man behind him was found out to have been a Hollister local: a film projectionist named Gus De Serpa. De Serpa was still alive, and he remembered the photograph well enough to set the surrounding scene back in motion. "I worked at the Granada Theater, which was on the corner of Seventh and San Benito," he said. "I would have got off work around 11 p.m. My wife came to pick me up, and we decided to walk up Main Street to see what was going on."

Over on Main Street, two men—Barney Peterson, a photographer, and a reporter named C. I. Dourghty, both of whom had just flown down from San Francisco—were scraping a pile of beer bottles together and arranging them, just so, around a motorcycle. "After a while," De Serpa recalled, a "drunk guy" came along.

"He was just in the vicinity, and he was pretty well loaded. There was a bar right there, Johnny's Bar. I think he came wandering out of that bar, and they just got him to sit down there. I told my wife, 'That's not right; they shouldn't be doing that. Let's stand behind them so they won't take the picture.' I figured if I was behind them they wouldn't take it. But he took a picture anyhow, this fellow did, he didn't care."

Peterson's fiction inspired others, including a short story, called "Cyclists' Raid," that ran in *Harper's* in 1951 and served as the basis of Stanley Kramer's film *The Wild One*—which starred Marlon Brando, along with Lee Marvin, and caused an immediate sensation upon its opening, a few days after Christmas, in 1953.

In America, Elvis Presley, and not a few rock-and-roll stars who came in his wake, adopted Brando's look (his blue jeans, his T-shirt, his black leather jacket), as well as his slouch and his mumble. In England, where *The Wild One* was banned for fourteen years, an aspiring rock group adapted and altered the name of Marvin's motorcycle club, the Beetles. And in Hollywood, *The Wild One* created an entire genre: *Motorpsycho!*, *The Wild Angels*, *Devil's Angels*, *Cycle Vixens*, *The Cycle Savages*, *Hell's Bloody Devils*, and *Hells Angels on Wheels* (with a young Jack Nicholson, who went on to star in the archetypal anti-biker-movie biker movie, *Easy Rider*) were just a few of the films that owed their existence to Stanley Kramer's production.* Kathryn Bigelow's first feature-length movie, *The Loveless*, was a moody, modern-day recasting of *The Wild One*; Mel Gibson's *Road Warrior* trilogy was a grand, postapocalyptic take on the formula. (In the *Mad Max* films, the whole continent of Australia gets taken over by bikers.) And if *The Road Warrior*'s aesthetic was a clear influence on the Rats' own, the Rats had cribbed from *The Wild One* in equally obvious ways. The club's rat skulls were based on the human skulls that Brando's bikers—members of the Black Rebels Motorcycle Club, or BRMC—wore on the backs of their jackets. There was even the happy alignment of acronyms:

---

*The old *Beach Party* movies, which starred Frankie Avalon and Annette Funicello, featured Harvey Lembeck as Eric Von Zipper, a motorcycle club president who dressed just like Brando's character in *The Wild One*. Von Zipper's club was called the Rat Pack and its members were called "the Rats"—although, in real life, a pack of rats is called a "mischief."

Trevor told me that, as it had been designed, the Rats' original logo had looked even more like the BRMC's, with pistons where the wrenches now were. He'd changed the design, he said, to look less like the logo used by the Outlaws—a real MC, which had formed in 1935 but changed its own logo (a winged motorcycle) when *The Wild One* came out, to look just like that of the BRMC's. This reminded me of the real-life gangsters who, in the seventies, had changed their appearance and affect to align more closely with the fiction Francis Ford Coppola (and, again, Brando) had set forth in *The Godfather*.

I asked Trevor, "How much do you know about the bikers who were actually there, in 1947?"

"A little," he said. "It's something we talk about. You pick up scraps, see things on TV or the Internet. But you pretty much have to piece it together. Whatever you find out, I'll be glad to know."

The motorcyclists who'd arrived in Hollister in 1947 had come for that year's Gypsy Tour rally. Sanctioned by the AMA and named for the motorcyclists who'd travel, sometimes for days, to get there, the Gypsy Tours were almost as old as organized motorcycling itself. In Hollister, a small agricultural town on the San Andreas fault line, ninety miles south of San Francisco and just outside of the old Spanish mission where Hitchcock would shoot parts of *Vertigo*, Gypsy Tours had been held before, over Fourth of July weekends, at a track on the outskirts of town. But the tours were suspended for the duration of America's involvement in the Second World War, and when Hollister's rally resumed, on July 3, 1947, the town's residents found that American motorcycling, and American motorcyclists, had changed. Thousands of gypsies who rode in that year behaved like the sportsmen had in the past: they booked rooms and registered for hill climbs, track races, and other AMA-sanctioned events. But a few hundred more stayed in town, partied, crashed out on the sidewalk beside their bikes, or bivouacked in parks or in haystacks. Some were Boozefighters—self-described members of "a drinking club with a motorcycle problem." They were the direct models for Brando's Black Rebels. Others belonged to the Galloping Geese, the Pissed Off Bastards of Bloomington, and the Market Street Commandos.

By most accounts, including their own, these were the clubs that had caused the most trouble. They fought and threw bottles, raced through the streets, rode their bikes into bars and restaurants. At one point, the Boozefighters plied a town drunk with wine, tied him to a wheelchair, and hooked the chair up to the back of a car. "I looked back and he had fallen out of the chair," the club's founder and president, "Wino" Willie Forkner, recalled. "So we put him on the hood and started driving again. Slowly. But he looked like he wasn't breathing, so we thought he was dead. We dropped him in an alley, covering him up with papers, and took off."

Wino Willie was the inspiration for Lee Marvin's character, Chino. And, despite Brando's influence, Chino became the true model for presidents of actual outlaw MCs. "When I saw *The Wild One*, Lee Marvin instantly became my hero," the Hells Angels' president, Sonny Barger, would say. "Chino was my man. Marlon Brando as Johnny was the bully. His boys rode Triumphs and BSAs and wore uniforms. Lee's attitude was 'If you fuck with me, I'll hit back.' Lee and his boys were riding fucked-up Harleys and Indians. I certainly saw more of Chino in me than Johnny. I still do."

Trevor thought the same thing, and put it to me more plainly: "Brando's so fucking gloomy," he said. "Who ever heard of a gloomy motorcycle club president?"

At the time of the Hollister rally, Wino Willie would have been a few days shy of his twenty-seventh birthday. During the war, he'd been a waist gunner on board a B-24 Liberator named the *Pacific Tramp*. Upon his return, his old club, 13 Rebels MC, had expelled him, presumably for drunkenness. (In *The Wild One*, Chino's been expelled from his old club, the BRMC.) According to legend, the 13 Rebels had asked Wino Willie to return his club sweater—and Forkner had shat in the sweater before doing so.

And so, Wino Willie was a degenerate: a perfect model for the man in Barney Peterson's photograph. But in all of the photos that I've seen, Forkner looks nothing at all like Peterson's drunkard. If anything, he's stylish, handsome: a dead ringer for Errol Flynn, right down to the pencil mustache. In fact, in every one of the photos that Peterson took in Hollister, aside from the obvious fakes, the motorcyclists are all young, good looking, and healthy. Their clubs could have passed for male modeling agencies. But for me, one photograph is especially striking. It's of a motorcyclist who's dressed in a black Schott Perfecto, a leather jacket that's all but identical to the one Brando will wear in *The Wild One*. He is remarkably handsome. His striped T-shirt's worn out, just so; his paint-splattered jeans are selvedge and expertly cuffed. He'd be uncommonly cool, with or without the two cops who are flanking him, holding his arms in stress positions, and marching him straight toward the camera.

Both of the cops are wearing jodhpurs: they seem to belong to some other century. The man they're arresting looks like a time traveler; someone who belongs on the screen, or in a Warhol silk screen.

No one looked like this in the forties.

It's a brilliant photo. Brando's costume designers must have studied it, doing nothing to alter the look, except for adding a cap (which bikers have largely ignored). Since then, the man's jeans and striped T-shirt have become the fashion world's default settings. His Schott Perfecto has been worn (though bikers themselves have moved on), not only by Brando and James Dean, but by Warhol, the Ramones, *Bad*-era Michael Jackson,

Tom of Finland, and the Japanese girlfriend in Jim Jarmusch's *Mystery Train*. And then there is the man's expression, which is proud and defiant in ways the time didn't allow for. Johnny, the man Brando played in *The Wild One*, isn't much for conversation; Chino gets much better lines. But at one point, a townsperson asks, "What're you rebelling against, Johnny?" Brando replies, "Whaddaya got?" It is the movie's most famous exchange. But the man under arrest in the photo could have told us exactly what he was rebelling against, and why. His is the earliest image I've seen of the postwar counterculture. And if I were to guess, I'd say he was a soldier, just back from the war.

The Galloping Geese, the Pissed Off Bastards of Bloomington, the Market Street Commandos, and the Boozefighters were all formed, in the war's immediate aftermath, by men who'd seen combat in Europe or in the Pacific Theater. For them, the clubs provided some measure of comfort, a means of re-creating the camaraderie of the barracks, and a reminder of the adrenaline that had gotten them through their missions. Some were experienced motorcyclists who'd raced on the AMA circuit. Others had learned to ride in the service and returned to find decommissioned Harleys waiting for them at auction. America put on a brave face to meet them—but it, too, had changed, in ways that the men would find hard to articulate. The phrase "shell shock" was used then to describe combat stress and its aftereffects. Everyone drank, and airmen like Willie Forkner were especially prone to hearing loss, which made it hard for them to land jobs upon their return.* The GI Bill provided

---

*One way to gauge the effects of service on World War II bomber crews would be to follow the career of Jimmy Stewart, who commanded several squadrons of B-24 Liberators and made twenty runs over Europe—a wartime résumé that helps to explain the "dark," haunted Stewart of postwar films like *The Naked Spur* and, especially, *Vertigo*.

veterans with loans, low-interest mortgages, and tuition benefits. But not everyone was cut out for college. "We were rebelling against the establishment," Forkner would say. "You go fight a goddamn war, and the minute you get back and take off the uniform and put on Levi's and a leather jacket they call you an asshole."

MCs that formed after the Second World War were militarized in ways that the original MCs had not been. The formations they rode in were arranged like squadrons; riders who brought up the rear were called "tail gunners." More and more members ditched their sweaters and bought jackets by Schott—the company that had supplied bomber crews with their bomber jackets. There was a certain comfort level with violence—which is what makes Brando's film come alive, though the screenplay never quite explains it.

In "Cyclists' Raid," the story that ran in *Harper's*, it's clear that all of the bikers are soldiers just back from the war. In *The Wild One*, the war is never mentioned. But at the time, fans would have remembered Brando's performance in his first film, *The Men*, which he had made for Stanley Kramer three years earlier, in 1950. In *The Men*, Brando plays a paralyzed veteran; to prepare, the actor spent four weeks in character with paraplegics at a veterans' hospital in Los Angeles, and was accepted by them as one of their own. And, for all intents and purposes, Johnny, in *The Wild One*, is the same character, kicked a bit further along down the line. Here, the wounds are internal, incommunicable. Ultimately, *The Wild One* takes the difficulty of articulating its subject (what war does) as its true subject.

Perhaps it's as simple as that: if war was the condition that gave rise to modern motorcycle clubs, then the reason that so many clubs—the Rats, the Hells Angels, the East Bay Dragons, and countless others—felt at home in Oakland was that, in Oakland, the war had never quite ended.

At the end of the First World War, demobilized soldiers had started race riots all over the country—so many that the summer of 1919 is remembered as the "Red Summer." At the end of the Second World War, demobilized soldiers took part in a strike wave so large that it looked, at times, like a rebellion. The numbers are staggering: in 1945 (when the country's population was just under 140 million), 3.47 million workers went out on strike. In 1946, 4.6 million workers went out on strike, and the towns of Rochester, New York; Stamford, Connecticut; and Lancaster, Pennsylvania, were shut down for days on end by general strikes—the last of which had taken place in Oakland.

Across the nation, veterans were returning, flooding the labor marketplace, and finding that prices had soared, while employers kept wartime wage freezes in place. Corporate profits hit an all-time high, but in Oakland, women who'd held good jobs in the shipyards found themselves scrambling for work in downtown's department stores—Breuner's, Capwell's, the White House, Roos Brothers, I. Magnin, Jackson's, Hastings, and Kahn's. These women waited for hours in basement "ready rooms," to see if they'd be called to work that day. Those who weren't called were sent home without pay. But on October 23, 1946, women workers at Hastings Department Store, one block from city hall on Latham Plaza, went on strike. On Halloween, they were joined by women who worked at Kahn's, across the street. A week later, the teamsters joined their pickets and refused to take goods into either store. Christmas was approaching; by the start of the shopping season, both stores were nearly empty.

A few blocks away, in the Tribune Tower, Joseph Knowland was watching. Under his direction, the city hired Veteran Truckers—a strikebreaking firm from Los Angeles. On December 1, Oakland police moved the firm's scab trucks through the pickets. While trying to stop them, a man named Newton Selvidge was run over by a three-wheeled OPD motorcycle. His injuries were the catalyst for a general strike that was called later that day.

Latham Square became the strike's epicenter. The police tried to wave streetcars through. The streetcar drivers did not oblige. They stopped the cars where they stood and removed their control boxes, blocking traffic entirely. Several times during the days that followed, the drivers, many of them veterans who'd turned their Eisenhower jackets into work uniforms, without removing the overseas bars that they'd earned, formed in military ranks and marched through the streets in support of the strikers. Except for deliveries of milk (which strikers allowed to continue), the city was all but shut down.

A street party formed in Latham Square, and strikers allowed the bars to stay open if bartenders agreed to put their jukeboxes out on the sidewalks. By the third day of the strike, 140,000 workers had walked out in solidarity with the strikers at Kahn's and Hastings. That evening, ten thousand workers met at Oakland Auditorium and held the biggest labor meeting in Bay Area history, while five thousand more stood outside, in the rain, and listened.

The strike ended on December 5, when union leaders overrode the rank and file and returned workers to their jobs. In return, the city agreed that it and the Oakland Police Department would stop using motorcycles for crowd control and would remain neutral in all future labor disputes. A sound truck was sent out to Latham Square to tell strikers they could go home, though none of their original demands had been met. A few months later—less than two weeks before the Hollister rally—Congress overrode Harry Truman's veto and enacted the Taft-Hartley Act.

Formally known as the Labor Management Relations Act, Taft-Hartley was a direct response to the strike wave and, especially, the strike in Oakland. Thanks to its measures, which included a ban on sympathy strikes, Oakland's general strike was the last one that ever took place on American soil. And if memories of the general strikes were still fresh and raw at the start of the Hollister rally, this made it easier to understand the decision, on the part of *Life*'s editors, to go with Barney Peterson's photograph of a drunkard—a slovenly figure; a prole—instead of an image that would have brought soldiers and strikers to mind. They showed us something revolting, instead of something that looked like revolt.

All of this was fresh in my mind when J.J. texted to tell me that the Rats had jumped him outside of Cole Coffee, and on my way out to meet him I stopped by the clubhouse, where many of the Rats had gathered. Big Mike was there. When I saw him I asked, "What really happened with J.J.?"

"It's not the biggest thing in the world," Big Mike told me. "We're trying to let him have a normal life, be a normal person, do normal shit. He's putting it in our faces, buzzing our guys, being dangerous on the roads. So we had a meeting, and I went to Cole's. He says, 'No! I go wherever the fuck I want.' I reach for his coffee, and he fucking kicks me in the gut. It's on from there. We end up tussling and falling over some people's breakfast plates. It's a full-on, maniac tussle. I cut my wrist open but didn't notice till later. There's an old man standing there, with a chair, and some middle-aged yuppie woman is yelling, 'Hit him!' It was beautiful, in its way. But the fighting was over quickly, and then we were in a stalemate, locked up, grappling, stuck at odds on the ground. I knew if I'd started to whale on him, I would get it from all these random people. But at that point, J.J. was ready to listen. His focus was there, and we ended up talking a bit. I don't know if everything became clear. But I know that he got a bit more of the message."

The message was, J.J. needed to lose his rat skull tattoo.

"I've been telling him for a long time," Mike said. "Two fucking years? You still got that fucking ink? The tattoo where he said, 'Make it bigger than Trevor's'? What kind of pussy shit is that, to begin with?"

I asked if Mike knew how long it would take to remove a tattoo that big.

"No idea," he said. "I've never had to fucking do it."

I thanked Mike for his time and drove down to J.J.'s house in the Lower Bottoms. He met me outside his garage, acting proud and wound up, but his story lined up, more or less, with Big Mike's.

"I could see him walking across the street," J.J. told me. "He had his vest on. I was just sitting there on the bench, up against the glass. He's like, 'You gotta leave, man.' I go, 'You can't tell me where I can and cannot be.' And he just jumped me. I was sitting down. I almost gave him an up-kick right in the mouth. We scuffled around for a little bit. Knocked over all of the tables in the fucking coffee shop. All of these local people from this nice little neighborhood are freaking out, screaming. 'Oh my God, guys! Stop, you're killing each other!'

"I pretty much caught every punch he threw at me. I tied his arms up. I got him in a headlock and we rolled around for maybe thirty seconds. Every punch he'd try to throw I'd either straight-arm or block it. He started getting exhausted, said I gotta get my tattoo removed. He was like, 'Get your goddamn tattoo removed, get out of the Bay Area, and quit trying to kill our folks on motorcycles.'

"I said, 'Hey, that shit's all in your head. I didn't try to kill anybody on a bike. I just pass them. They don't go that fast. Sorry.' He goes, 'You're gonna go, or we're gonna go. And I'm gonna see you tomorrow.'"

"Are you going to see him tomorrow?"

"I don't want to see any of those guys."

"How are you feeling?" I asked.

"A little sad, man. I could've knifed him. I could've broken his arm. I could've poked his eye out. All these things are what you do when you're fighting for your life."

"And the tattoo?"

"I'm getting it taken off. That's the thing. They keep saying I'm not, but every two months I get it blasted with the laser blaster. It gets me sick. The ink goes all the way through my body. But I'm doing it. They say that I'm not because they need ammunition to tell everybody that I'm a bad guy."

I asked him to show me.

J.J. nodded and took his shirt off. He turned around. And where the tattoo had been I saw a faint outline. The rat skull was still visible. But no one would have mistaken it for a tattoo. It looked much more like a wound.

The skin around it was soft, like baby's skin.

In time, I assumed, the scar tissue would form.

CHAPTER FOURTEEN

At some point, he told me, he'd done jobs involving lawn work. But the only real work that I saw Trevor do was at the Ruby Room, where he checked IDs, kept the peace, and managed the schedules and inventory. He drank tea while he worked, read books, and texted. Often, friends would come by. But most of the Rats drank at other bars now, and Trevor had plenty of time to himself. Whenever I'd drop by to see him, talk turned to the future: the houses he'd build and the babies he'd raise, once he had found the right woman. In the meanwhile, he said, he'd raise rabbits, to kill and to eat, on a large plot of land that he'd bought in the hills behind Livermore, together with Zhiva, the Rat, who got a small house on the property while Trevor took over an abandoned Airstream nearby. To get there from Livermore, you drove down long, twisty roads, opened an unmarked gate, locked the gate, crossed over a dried-out creek bed, guessed right at the fork, and took a winding trail up toward the overgrown hilltop. A view of the valley, when the trees cleared: Zhiva's house was right on top of it. But Zhiva's house was a windowless shell, which the previous owners had used as a pot grow, and Trevor's Airstream was busted and rotten. The upside was that no one lived nearby or complained when Trevor shot off his guns. Before long, he'd started to talk about a second house, higher up on the hill—one that he'd build himself and fill up with children.

"Where will they go to school?"

"I'm homeschooling," said Trevor.

"What about work?"

"I'll put them to work."

"Your work—"

"At the bar? We'd have to drive home in the dark."

Another thing Trevor imagined was that he would go back to law school.

I said, "You've never been to law school!"

"Not to become a lawyer. I'd be a go-between between lawyers and bikers who wanted to sue."

"For what?"

"For whatever they wanted to sue for."

"Why would you go to law school to do that?"

"I don't know. It couldn't hurt."

Trevor did not end up becoming a lawyer. But he did get the rabbits, bought from a ranch that supplied them to restaurants. He built cages, cared for the animals, and spent the rest of his time on the land clearing brush and shooting. There were rattlesnakes up in the hills; the first time I heard one, I thought that Trevor had turned over a beehive. But Trevor carried a shotgun around and didn't seem overly bothered. "Yep," he would say. "It's a snake."

We'd drive out on weekdays, once every week or so, before the start of Trevor's Ruby Room shifts. Lucy and I had a little convertible—an old green two-seater—and Trevor and I took the twisty turns fast. Up on the land, I'd turn a few old crates over while Trevor tacked paper targets to trees. Both of us shot lefty, though both of us favored our right. Both of us turned out to have weaker right eyes.

The time passed: two weeks, three weeks, then a month as we waited for Trevor's rabbits to multiply. Oddly, none of them were eaten. (There were mountain lions up there, as well.) But although they looked healthy, none of the rabbits had given birth. One day, Trevor sexed the adults—he never had at the outset—and we discovered that they were all males.

In the city I spent time with Jim Saleda, the Oakland cop I'd met through Trevor and the Rats. Jim was also a biker. Los Carnales, the club he belonged to, was made up entirely of law enforcement officers. All of them rode Harleys, and many were veterans. Jim's partner, James Beere, had taken time off from the police force to fight in and around Fallujah, and returned with a Bronze Star with a Combat V for Valor; whenever talk turned to the war Jim Saleda would say, "Now, Jim Beere's a real hero." But Saleda had also served, aboard submarines as a young man, and in the Army Reserve in Iraq where, southeast of Baghdad, he'd been injured in an IED explosion.

"I met the Rats through Jim Beere, when I came home from Iraq," he told me. "It was the way it had been with war vets from generations before, the way they reminded me of my brothers from Iraq. They accepted me for what I was, and although I was a cop, none of them asked me for favors."

Saleda had a young daughter, who had been bullied at her Oakland school. One day, the Rats had arrived, in formation, in front of the building to let other kids, parents, and the administration know that the girl was not to be bothered. The Rats had also been there when Saleda's son passed, suddenly, at the age of twenty-two. The funeral had been a sight, Jim told me, with Los Carnales MC and police department motorcycles leading the procession, and a chapel full of the Rats. "They'd offered to help me get stuff from my son's apartment," he said. "I called them the morning that we'd planned to do it, but they had already done it—two hours earlier, so that I wouldn't have to."

I knew, already, that Trevor liked and respected Saleda. But I'd come to see that Jim genuinely loved Trevor and the rest of the Rats.

Jim was out on disability now, waiting for his retirement, which was a few months away. He had already moved his wife and daughter out to the country in Minnesota, where his wife's people were—after her first day of school, Jim's daughter had called and said, "Daddy, there are no bullies here." Now, packed to join them, he counted the hours until his last day on the force.

"You know, " he told me, "we hired a bunch of dot-commers, after the last bubble burst. For a lot of these people, policing is a job. But policing is not a job. It's a calling, a vocation. These fuckers, they work five years, get vested, all of a sudden get hurt, and retire with fifty percent of their pension. Me, I did twenty hard fucking years in this city, almost. I'm going to walk away with fifty-five percent of my pension, and my health's shot."

The work really had hollowed him out. Jim's face was gaunt. His beard and his hair had turned gray. "My cognitive's not what it once was," he told me when I asked about the IED he'd survived.

"I used to read," he said.

"Read what?" I asked.

"I used to like Dickens."

The biker bar we'd meet at was called Godspeed. Jim lived nearby, off of San Pablo, and would walk down to the bar. I'd drive, and keep an eye on my drinking as I asked about Jim's life as a cop. He answered my questions on the condition that nothing would see its way into print until his retirement had gone through.

In 2003, Oakland's police force had been placed under federal supervision—fallout from a case (known as the "Riders" scandal) in which four Oakland cops had (or had not) kidnapped, beaten, and/or framed a series of innocent (or not-so-innocent) residents of West Oakland. One of the policemen had escaped to Mexico—quite possibly with the help of other police department members. The other three were fired but later acquitted in court. In the end, the city had settled with 119 plaintiffs (all of them black) who'd filed civil rights lawsuits. One result, Saleda told me, was that morale in the police department had plummeted.

"Cops don't get out of their cars," he said. "They're afraid of complaints, afraid of getting fired. My God, to stop somebody in this day and age, it's five or six pieces of paper! There are more cops now in internal affairs than there are on the homicide squad. To give an example, consider my neighbor. Let's say she's a little off. She thinks I'm shooting gamma rays at her, drilling holes in her ceiling, watching her with cameras. If she knew I was a cop, and went down and filed a complaint against me for 'shooting gamma rays,' I'd get investigated, and it would go in my record. That's a big specter to carry around. And the bad guys in Oakland have learned that, because every complaint is investigated—even the ridiculous ones—they can single out the best cops, hammer them. Have all their buddies come in and make different complaints. All of a sudden, that cop's off the streets."

At the same time, the number of investigations the police themselves carried out had shrunk. Baltimore, which was not quite twice the size of Oakland, had five times as many cops. Detroit, which was just a bit larger, had four times as many. In

Oakland, six hundred cops covered the city's thirty-five beats in three shifts, riding in Lincoln units (one-man cars) that covered one beat, or in Adam units (two-man cars) that covered two. "Best-case scenario," Jim explained, "thirty-five beats equaled thirty-five cops. That never happened due to vacations, or people off sick or injured."

I did the math in my head: at any given time in Oakland, there were fewer cops on the streets than there were East Bay Rats. How was it possible, I asked, to patrol the city with a team the size of an army platoon?

"Adapt and overcome," Jim said. "You have to do the job with what you have. Innocent people depend on it. Their lives depend on it, and our own lives. But at the same time, our computers don't work. Our cars are ancient. The radios don't work. You asked me earlier about morale? There's no fucking morale. In the old days, people would be upbeat, joking in the locker room. Now they walk around with their heads down."

Some Rats had gotten the idea that, because I was a writer, there were aspects of their world that I could explain better than they themselves could have explained them. In a limited sense, they were right. They'd ask me about Oakland, the history of certain buildings or neighborhoods. They'd ask about city politics, the goings-on at city hall. And because I *was* a writer, with a library card and my days more or less to myself, I could usually answer their questions. The Rats still introduced me to people I hadn't yet met by telling them I was "embedded." I still avoided the phrase. But I did begin to think of myself as a sort of unofficial historian-in-residence, and it was in that capacity that I became interested in Yusuf Bey, in Your Black Muslim Bakery, and in the murder trial that involved Bey—a case that the Rats felt connected to via their physical proximity to the Bakery (which had been a mosque and a criminal organization as well as an actual bakery out on San Pablo, four blocks away from Godspeed), and their friendship with Jim Saleda.

The murder trial had begun a few months after my arrival in Oakland. After hearing about it from Trevor, I'd gone down to the Alameda County courthouse, around the corner from the Ruby Room, to sit in on the proceedings. But Trevor did not tell me, and I did not know at first, that Jim had been deeply involved in the buildup to the case.

The story was convoluted; the trial would last for the better part of a year. But it had begun simply enough, nearly a decade earlier, on June 20, 2002. On that day, a thirty-two-year-old woman had walked into OPD headquarters, gone up to the desk sergeant on duty, and asked to fill out a complaint against Yusuf Bey—a religious leader with one hundred "wives," give or take, in the City of Oakland, dozens of acknowledged children (six of whom were named "Yusuf" and numbered accordingly), and deep ties to local politicians.

On Soul Beat, a public-access TV channel that served Oakland's African American community, Bey preached hour-long sermons, on his own show, about black empowerment, superiority, and separatism, denouncing Jews and homosexuals and railing against the race of "blue-eyed devils" that controlled America's power structure. The rhetoric was in line with that of Elijah Muhammad's Nation of Islam, and while the Bakery itself was not affiliated, officially, with the Nation, Bey hung portraits of Muhammad up in his buildings and subscribed to the Nation's dietary precepts. At the Bakery, he served bean pies, fish sandwiches, and tofu burgers, and by most accounts the food was good, though the service could be a bit spotty.

"They liked white girls," I was told by a white girl who used to grab lunch at the Bakery. "A white guy who came in, they'd ignore him at best."

Nevertheless, during his first run for the mayor's office in Oakland, in the late nineties, Jerry Brown had sought Bey's endorsement. Ron Dellums, who'd served as chairman of the House Armed Services Committee (and went on to succeed Brown as mayor) had been a prominent supporter of Bey, along with Congresswoman Barbara Lee, and the leader of the California State Senate, Don Perata, had helped the Bakery get concessions at the Oakland Stadium, where the Oakland A's played, and at the Oakland Airport. Despite rumors that Bey and his associates at the Bakery were linked to various criminal activities, the Bakery had also been contracted to provide security services for public schools in Oakland.

Dressed in suits and bow ties (clip-ons, which came off easily in altercations), the same associates could be seen drilling, in tight military formations, on Oakland streets.

At the same time, there were rumors that Bakery members had been involved in beatings and killings, extortion, and fraud. There was also a rumor that OPD had stay-away orders regarding Bakery operations. Several cops told me that this wasn't strictly the case: "Discouraged from looking too closely" would have been a better description, they said. But Jim Saleda told me that when the woman who'd come into OPD headquarters had made her intentions clear, the desk sergeants had ducked for cover.

"She came in to the front desk," Jim said. "Everyone freaked out. I said, 'I'll go down and talk to her.' Then I started to build a case. It took a few months, but we hit Yusuf Bey with twenty-seven felonies."

Jim couldn't tell me much more; he didn't know whether or not he'd be called to testify at the trial. But the report he'd written was in the public record—I dug it up—and found that it read like a novel:

The Victim said she came to know the Suspect through her father, who worked for and was a member of the Suspect's Mosque. The Victim's father worked at the Suspect's bakery. The Victim said that her father, his girlfriend (Joan Lewis), and her brother and sister lived in property owned by the Suspect (5832 San Pablo Ave, Your Black Muslim Bakery). The Victim said that during this time period the Suspect on occasion would fondle her and rub up against her.

The Victim said that at some point she and her siblings came under the care of the Suspect and his wife, Suspect #2 (Noor Bey). The Victim said she lived with the Suspects at 1079 59th St. The Victim said that the Suspect had gone on a trip to Guyana. The Victim said that he returned from this trip in the middle of the night. The Victim said that the Suspect came to her room and sodomized her. The Victim said she told Suspect #2 about the incident and Suspect #2 said to her that the Suspect is not doing anything to her (the Victim) that he didn't do to me (Suspect #2). The Victim was about ten years old at the time of this incident.

The Victim said that the Suspect continued to molest her from the time she was eight years old until the time she was able to get away from him, when she was eighteen years old. The Victim said during this time the Suspect sodomized her 3–4 times, had vaginal intercourse with her too many times to count, and made her perform oral sex on him numerous times.

The Victim said that while she lived with the Suspect she was not allowed to go to school and was forced to work all day at the Bakery. The Victim said at one point she complained to a social worker about not being able to go to school. The Suspect told the social worker that the Victim did go to school and she, the social worker believed them.

The Victim said she was punished for telling the social worker that she was not going to school, by being forced to get up hours early every day and read a book.

The Victim said that the Suspect was the biological father of all three of her children. The Victim said she is certain that the Suspect is her children's father and it was impossible for them to be another person's children. The Victim said that her oldest child is now twenty years old (■■■■) and that he was conceived when she was twelve or thirteen years old. The Victim said she also has an eighteen-year-old daughter by the Suspect and a fifteen-year-old son. The Victim said that all of her children were the result of the Suspect's molestation of her.

The Victim's children are:
1) ■■■■ MB 18 June 82
2) ■■■■ FB 02 May 84
3) ■■■■ MB 08 Jan 87

There had been other crimes: kidnappings, assaults, murders that may have dated back to, or preceded, the Zebra Killings—a series of attacks, all taking place in the seventies, in which Black Muslims shot whites at random or hacked them to death with machetes. (Art Agnos, a future mayor of San Francisco, was the victim of one such attack; he was shot twice in the back and survived. In his book *Killing the Messenger*, Bay Area journalist Thomas Peele makes a case for Yusuf Bey's involvement in the Zebra Killings.) Bey had used his connections to defraud the city in various ways. "We all knew they were organized crime," Jim told me. "It was common knowledge that they were dirty. But they were also protected, not by OPD, but by people at various levels of power. They were gangsters, equivalent to the political machines of the wards of Chicago in the twenties and thirties."

And yet, it had been a shock to discover that Bey had also been farming children—collecting the benefits paid to kids that he'd asked his wives to adopt. For him, the rapes seem to have been a fringe benefit: a means of control, and a way of manufacturing more children, who were then raped in turn. Bey had beaten these children, urinated on them, defecated in their mouths. Throughout, he had threatened them—said that he'd kill them, and their families, if they told anyone outside of the Bakery about the abuse. When the children turned to Bey's wives for help, the wives said that his actions had all been the will of Allah. Complaints received by the county's Department of Child Protective Services were not ignored, completely. But in every instance, CPS workers chose to believe Bey's side of the story, or interviewed the victims in his presence.

The woman who'd given Jim her statement had gone to OPD headquarters because she had found out, that day, that Bey had begun to molest a daughter that she'd had with him.

Jim managed to obtain DNA evidence that backed her claims. But Bey had died of colon cancer (or, it was rumored, of AIDS) while awaiting trial—at which point, the story of Your Black Muslim Bakery turned, almost immediately, from pure civic tragedy to something resembling a full-on Shakespearean bloodbath.

Less than a year after Bey's death, in 2003, his financial adviser and chosen successor, Waajid Aljawwaad Bey, failed to show up for work at the Bakery; his body was later discovered in a shallow grave in the Oakland Hills. Following a power struggle, Yusuf Bey's twenty-two-year-old son Antar took control. But in 2005, Antar was gunned down at a North Oakland filling station, and leadership passed to Yusuf Bey IV (known as "Fourth"). Still in his teens, Fourth was soon seen, in CCTV footage, busting up West Oakland's liquor stores. Together with men from the Bakery, he arrived at San Pablo

Liquor Store, across the street from the Victory Warehouse, beat up the clerks, and smashed the store's merchandise. Then the men walked to New York Market, a liquor store a few blocks away, beat up another clerk, and stole a pump-action shotgun.

Fourth was arrested several times in the months that followed, but not for those crimes. In Vallejo, he was arrested for using a fake ID to get a no-money-down loan on a Mercedes-Benz. In San Francisco, he was arrested for trying to run down a strip club bouncer. Back in Vallejo, he was arrested for using a fake ID to open a savings account; police there found an unregistered gun in his car. In between the arrests, he bought several luxury cars, all using fake IDs; faked notary stamps; forged a judge's signature; and, together with a few associates, secured sub-prime mortgages on several houses.

At the time, the Bakery was hundreds of thousands of dollars behind in its taxes and in arrears on a mortgage Antar had taken out on the Bakery's headquarters. Fourth filed for bankruptcy. He was facing a charge of attempted murder, for the incident in San Francisco. A warrant for his arrest had already been issued. But OPD didn't know, yet, that Fourth had also been killing people in Oakland. On July 8, 2007, a thirty-one-year-old homeless man named Odell Roberson was shot several times, with an assault rifle, around the corner from the Bakery. Four days later, a thirty-six-year-old restaurant worker named Michael Wills was killed, also with an assault rifle, a few blocks away on San Pablo Avenue. And on August 2, a reporter named Chauncey Bailey, who was working on a piece about the Bakery, was assassinated, in broad daylight, in downtown Oakland, as he walked to his job at a small African American weekly called the *Oakland Post*.

It was the first time in more than three decades that an

American journalist had been killed for reporting a domestic story.

On the day he was killed, Chauncey Bailey had on a suit that he'd bought at a thrift store. His assassin, a Bakery associate named Devaughndre Broussard, wore black shoes and black pants, a black T-shirt, gloves, and a black hoodie. He carried a shotgun and wore a ski mask that covered the bottom half of his face. Bailey was a few months shy of his fifty-eighth birthday. Broussard was nineteen years old.

The first shots hit Bailey in his upper body. Broussard turned and ran, then turned back around, as if he'd forgotten something. Then he ran back and shot Bailey, once more, in the face. The weapon he used was the shotgun that Yusuf Bey's men had taken from the clerk at New York Market.

Most of these facts came out in the course of Broussard's testimony, delivered over several days at the Alameda County courthouse, three years later, in 2011. I'd been attending the trial for weeks already, sitting behind reporters who had gathered and a scattering of old men who sat in the back row, like gallows birds, and who'd decided to attend the trial for want of anything better to do. They seemed to feel right at home in the courtroom, but nothing I'd ever seen had prepared me for Broussard, who was fidgety on the stand, giggling nervously as he recounted specifics. His laughter gave me just enough time to jot exchanges with the DA down in my legal pad:

"Once you got into the street did you turn around and go back to where Mr. Bailey was?"
"Yes."
"Why?"
"To make sure he dead."

"Did you think that shooting him twice with a shotgun, he would not already be dead?"

"Three times would have made it for certain."

It had occurred to me, during our encounter with the Oakland bus stop, that my friend Trevor might have been a sociopath. I did not know that this was the case—I was not a psychologist— and I did not know if knowing for sure would have changed my opinion of Trevor: if it would have made him seem weirder to me, or less weird. But I'd seen enough to go canvass for other opinions.

"Trevor is so passive, in such a broad way," Jason Lockwood had told me. "He's extremely passive. It's one of the reasons that I find him interesting, the fact that I still can't describe his personality. But I can tell you one story. There was an altercation, once, at the bar. We were escorting this guy out, and the guy spun around and rushed Trevor. I grabbed one of his arms, just trying to stop him. And the guy did calm down. He put his arms down, I dropped my arms. And then this guy tackled me with, like, a football tackle. Straight at the hips, ran me back, and slammed me through a door.

"Now, I was wearing all of my motorcycle gear, minus my helmet, so I didn't feel a thing. I tied up one arm, got the guy in a headlock, shouldered him against the wall. Trevor kind of sauntered back, like nothing was going on. He's dealing with the bar lights and the door, getting everything back to the way it was. But when I looked down, I saw that he had one of those loop knives, with his fingers looped through it. He didn't make a big deal out of it. But if this guy broke free, well, I guess we were going to stab him.

"Normally, in a fight, I've learned to watch the other guy's eyes. It doesn't matter if you're scared or not, your pupils are going to get bigger. But in this case, I remember, I looked straight into Trevor's eyes and saw no change at all. Is that sociopathic? I wouldn't know. But I did find it to be very strange."

Jason's story came back to me as I sat, for days on end, and listened to Broussard's testimony. The longer I listened, the saner Trevor came to seem. But then I also took note of the similarities: The cracked, broken homes that had defined their backgrounds. The pull toward some sort of family, however makeshift, slapped-together, and flawed. The casual acceptance of bloodshed. To greater and lesser extents, these were things that the Rats I had gotten to know had in common. Even Jason—the most well-adjusted Rat I had met, with his steady job and his mortgage, the son he was committed to, utterly—had said as much.

"When I was prospecting," Lockwood had told me, "a girl I knew asked me, 'Why? When you're so nice and normal?' Norton Aaron was like, 'No, he's not. You may not be able to see it, but if he wants to be in an MC, there's something wrong with him.' That was true. Probably, everyone in the world is fucked up, in one way or another, but anyone who's attracted to a fraternal, brotherhood-type thing is going to feel like there's something missing, and probably has been missing, from their lives. Usually not something savory, I'd guess."

Jason had had his own terrible childhood—not an unusual thing among the Rats, though Jason's had been unusually bad. When he was little, his mother had whisked him away from Kansas and Jason's abusive father, and brought him out to Oakland. It was the 1970s, the height of what Jason called the "black backlash era," and Jason was one of the few white kids in his school. He was beaten up on a near-daily basis.

"I got jumped constantly," he told me. "It was ridiculous, unbelievable. I was amazed, even at the time, at how old some of the other kids were. I was like, 'There's no way you should be hitting someone this small.'"

By his teens, Jason had turned into a punk rocker. He got into drugs and spent more and more time away from home. By then, his dad had long since reappeared in the Bay Area. But Jason's father was deranged, suicidal, and one day (Jason was fifteen days shy of his fifteenth birthday) a jogger had found him hanging from a tree, up in the Berkeley Hills.

After the suicide, Jason had shut down completely. He'd been on and off running away from his home already. Now he began to squat, full-time, with other runaways in San Francisco. He became a skinhead. And, soon afterward, he became a racist thug.

"I lived with some guys who sold drugs and gave me scraps of stuff to sell to other people," he recalled. "I'd make enough money off that to get around. I didn't have a lot of expenses. Pizza and beer, an occasional punk show. Then me and a few other guys started the first skinhead gang in San Francisco. We realized that 'Bay Area Skin Heads' spelled 'BASH'—and we thought that was funny. But, of course, with a group of teenage boys, someone's going to take it seriously. It took us two or three months to decide we were going to be Nazi skinheads. In the beginning, that wasn't too serious, either. Then, at some point, it did turn serious."

Friends of mine who'd grown up in the Bay Area still remembered the BASH Boys, as they had been known. Jason and his friends had broken up parties, beaten people badly, and done worse things in the shadows.

"In retrospect," Jason said, "that was the worst period of my life. I spent all of my time scared that I would get dragged into fights. I didn't want to be in fights. All of the fights I had been in had been twenty guys that were stomping on me. But then, I figured out—'Hey, look, it's a bunch of us stomping on others!' It was off-the-cuff racism, for lack of a better term. We'd go out looking for people. We hated homeless guys. We were homeless, too, so we were in direct competition with them.

And, I won't lie about this, there was definitely a focus on black guys. But I'd grown up in Oakland and Berkeley, places that were so liberal, and so integrated, that I couldn't go back and look at the people I had grown up with, had been friends with since I was a kid, and decide that they were pieces of shit. I had one interaction with a Jewish friend—he snatched a card I was passing out out of my hand, tore it in half, asked me what I was doing. At the age of fifteen, I knew and understood that the Nazis had killed a lot of Jewish people. But it hadn't hit home for me that this friend had a grandmother with a tattoo on her arm. We had a little scuffle, and I remember being surprised at how angry he was. Didn't everyone think it was funny? Wasn't it all a big joke?"

In the end, cops in San Francisco put Jason on a bus back to Oakland. "Get the fuck out of town," they told him. "We're not going to chaperone you idiots around."

"That was such a relief," Jason said. "I'm not a tough guy, and that's my picture of a tough guy—someone who's proving himself all the time. Someone who can't be polite because that would be weak. I'd never go back to any of it. And that played into a lot of my hesitation over the Rats. It took an arm and a leg to get me to join. I kept putting it off, coming up with excuses. I was not about to go back to living that way, spending all day, every day, worrying about being angry. It's such an emotional drain; you can't live an adult life and be like that. When your parents are as batty as mine were, the craziest things come to seem normal. You don't know any better. And then, one day, you're not a kid anymore. You realize things could have been different. You know that you can't go around exploding all the time and also be happy."

Back in the East Bay, Jason had gotten off drugs. He took up karate, dropped in and out of high school, and worked a long series of menial jobs. "I didn't drink or do anything else for a decade," he told me. "That whole time was martial arts and service jobs. I got into IT when I was twenty-six. But I'd been moving in that direction ever since I had started doing martial arts. That gave me a way to get the energy out, and to get out from under the feeling of feeling threatened, and helpless, and reacting in a really bad way to everything because everything really was so threatening all of the time."

I am a Jew. And up to the moment that Jason told me his story, I never would have imagined that I'd find myself relating to, much less liking, someone who'd identified, openly, as a Nazi. But the more Jason talked—about his shitty childhood, what it had done to him, and what he'd done to overcome the things he'd done to others—the more I found myself thinking about Trevor's childhood, and my own. About all of the ways we'd been warped, and how far we still had to go before we could undo the warping. We'd had our twenties and thirties to work on ourselves. We were white, and the advantages that whiteness brings had had time to kick in. And yet, we still found ourselves drawn to extremes. Even we loners—outliers like Jason and Trevor, and me—had been drawn, for our various reasons, to a club that revolved around violence. And none of us had had it as bad as Devaughndre Broussard, who'd committed his worst crimes while still in his teens and would be spending his twenties and thirties in prison.

Broussard had struck a deal with the state—twenty-five years in exchange for his testimony against Fourth and a Bakery associate named Antoine Mackey, who were being tried together. He had no obvious incentives to lie. He knew that any lie would endanger the deal he had made. As a result, those of us in the courtroom had as much access to Broussard's mind, and his motivations, as the DA's questions could grant us.

This turned out to be a great deal of access, and Broussard

had an odd mind. He'd been kept alone, in protective custody, for several years. On the witness stand, he would talk to himself, babble under his breath, maybe pray; it was impossible to tell. At times, his head would roll backward. He'd answer the simplest questions by saying, "I'm not understanding that." But then, suddenly, he'd respond to some challenge and snap to attention, and when this happened, he'd show himself to be surprisingly bright. The DA called him "a sociopath, who had no sympathy, no feelings." She called him "a stone-cold killer." Sometimes, she said, "you have to make a deal with a demon to get to the devil." What she meant was that Broussard was a demon, and Fourth was the devil she was out to capture. But Broussard was a strange sort of demon.

As a child, Broussard had grown up with drug dealers. He'd shuttled between friends and relatives. At the age of eighteen, on a bus in San Francisco, he'd snatched an art student's iPod. He'd punched the student, kicked him, and gotten away. But, it turned out, his victim was the nephew of a political operative in the city. Broussard was picked up soon afterward and ended up in the county jail, where he had had the misfortune of hearing about Your Black Muslim Bakery.

The Bakery employed ex-convicts, Broussard was told. The Beys were always looking for people like him. He called the Bakery upon his release, and Fourth gave him a room with no bed, no water, and no electricity. He told Broussard that the Bakery needed soldiers—men "who were down for whatever." He made several promises, involving loans and credit hookups that Broussard could get. Even at the time, the promises had seemed ridiculous. And yet, Broussard had seen the cars Fourth was driving.

"Dude put you on about the credit," he said. "You can get your credit fixed up and you can make a lot of moves when you got your credit for good."

Broussard wanted the credit hookup.

At first, he washed pots and pans at the Bakery and worked security at strip malls and in clubs that the Bakery had contracts with. It was shit work, and Fourth put off paying him. But Broussard needed the job, not just for the money (which he wasn't getting) but so that he'd have something to show his probation officer in San Francisco. Broussard had a sleepy expression; a childhood nickname, which he hated, was "Catfish." He had a stutter. He didn't know who else would have hired him. Nevertheless, he'd quit the Bakery, twice. At one point, he'd tried to sell T-shirts to tourists at Fisherman's Wharf. But this was not the sort of work that his probation officer was satisfied with, and both times Broussard ended up back at the Bakery. "I was like putting applications and stuff," he would say. "And I knew who would hire me immediately: the Bakery. So, right, back to the Bakery."

When Broussard returned, for good, in June 2007, Chauncey Bailey had just been made editor of the *Oakland Post*.

Fourth partnered Broussard up with Mackey—another soldier, recently hired from San Francisco. Mackey was a bit older than Broussard; he'd survived three shootings already, and at least one stabbing, and had been registered as a sex offender at the age of thirteen. They got along well enough, and a little while later Broussard discovered that Odell Roberson—the homeless man who'd often been seen at the Bakery asking for handouts—was an uncle of the man who had shot Fourth's brother Antar.

"Me and Yusuf was outside in front of the Bakery, talking one morning," Broussard said. "Odell come down the street and he ask like, 'How you brothers doing?'"

Bey had said, "How are you doing, my brother?"

Roberson had said, "Can I get something to eat?"

To Broussard's amazement, Bey had given Roberson a fish sandwich.

"I was like, 'Y'all didn't do nothing? Y'all not going to do nothing about it?' "

It took Broussard a while to build up to the story of Roberson's death—which was the first murder he had committed on Fourth's behalf. The details were gruesome, when he got around to them. But the lead-up to the story is the thing that stuck in my mind, and Trevor's, when I read aloud from the notes I had taken in court.

"Is this a script?" Trevor asked me.

"No, man. This is verbatim from the trial."

"And the lawyer?"

"This is Mackey's lawyer, cross-examining Broussard, the hit man."

"And he's for real?"

"Well, he's very old, past retirement age, hard of hearing. For sure, he's out of his depth. But I think that he's trying, as best he can, to help his client."

"It sounds like a Laurel and Hardy exchange."

"It does push up against the limits of language."

"Read me the part about rabbits again?"

"This is the lawyer speaking: 'I want to go to a comment you made when you and Yusuf Bey IV were talking about, or your testimony that you were talking about, Mr. Roberson and why he hadn't been—why he wasn't dead yet, basically. Okay? Do you know what I'm talking about?' "

"This is the lawyer speaking?"

"Yes."

"And what does Broussard say?"

"He says, 'What do you mean?' "

"Okay," said Trevor. "Keep reading."

" 'Do you remember,' says the lawyer, 'when Mr. Roberson asked for a sandwich?'

"'Yes,' says Broussard.

"'Isn't it true that when Mr. Roberson asked for a sandwich that Mr. Bey gave him a sandwich?'

"'Yes.'

"'Okay. And then you commented to Mr. Bey, you made some kind of comment about "rabbits," didn't you?'

"'No.'

"'Okay.'

"'Those are thoughts.'

"'Those are thoughts that you had to yourself?'

"'Yes.'

"'Okay. So you thought to yourself that Yusuf Bey should do something about Mr. Roberson?'

"'No.'

"'What were the thoughts you had about rabbits?'

"'It was because from the impression that I had of Yusuf Bey IV, that if somebody would do something to his, he would do something to theirs. And here's this guy that is continuously around his neighborhood or the area to where he be's at daily, and so he was just walking around, and I thought of it in a context of a person who's hungry or who's starving and there's a rabbit 'round or a bunch of rabbits—well, shit, there go a rabbit. You can get one!'

"'There are rabbits, go get one?'

"'Yeah.'"

Here, Trevor interrupted. "Fourth found Broussard and this other guy, Mackey, in San Francisco?"

"Recruited them in San Francisco, yes."

"And the Bakery had already pretty much fallen apart?"

"Pretty much. Most people had split. But now Fourth has these two guys—"

"Who are like, what kind of chicken-shit shop are you running?"

"Pretty much."

"Forcing Fourth's hand?"

"Most likely."

"Okay. Keep reading."

" 'Because,' Broussard's saying, 'you can eat rabbits.' "

Trevor whistled and walked away to check on his own rabbits, which were still there, in their cages, failing to multiply. When he came back, I skipped down a few lines and continued.

" 'I was saying,' Broussard is saying, 'the way I was relaying it to myself is: Okay, if the person's hungry or starving and there's a bunch of rabbits around the area, so it shouldn't be nothing holding you back from satisfying your hunger by just killing one of the rabbits, so you can just eat a rabbit.'

" 'Instead of asking for a fish sandwich? Is that what you mean?' "

I looked up and saw Trevor staring at me. "At this point," I said, "the judge interrupted: 'No. It has nothing to do with Mr. Roberson. You're confused.' The DA held up a napkin she'd been doodling on. There was a rabbit on it, and a carrot, along with the words 'It's an analogy.' The lawyer saw it and said, 'It's an analogy?' "

" 'Yes,' said the judge."

" 'Ah,' said the lawyer."

" 'A figure of speech,' said the judge."

"Let me see that," said Trevor, who had grown impatient. In my notes, the transcript went on for several more pages, all of them in the same vein. As he flipped through, Trevor whistled again.

"Why did they kill the reporter?"

"They thought he was working on a story about the Bakery."

"Was he?"

"I think so."

"And the other guy?"

"Michael Wills. It looks like they killed him because Fourth and Mackey were driving around, in the middle of the night, talking about the Zebra Killings. Then they saw a white guy."

"Where?"

"By the Golden Gate School, up on San Pablo. Then they said, 'There's one!'"

"A white guy?"

"Yes."

"And they killed him?"

"A horrible story."

"And none of this would have happened if Broussard's probation officer hadn't made him go back to the Bakery?"

"Not quite. But I think Broussard felt boxed in."

"I'm sure Fourth did, too, after hiring these guys. Killers turn on you when you don't use them."

"Like I said, it's a horrible story," I said.

The trial went on for a few more months: there was the slow procession of witnesses, coroners, and police technicians; the jurors, who looked like a Greek chorus but never spoke; the rituals by which we were ushered in and out of the courtroom, instructed by bailiffs to turn off our cell phones, sit, stand, and silence ourselves—all of these things were theatrical, in ways that brought all of the old clichés about trials and theatrical productions to mind. There was the way that Fourth and his codefendant, Mackey, entered the courtroom, through a side door, like actors. Sometimes, during moments before court was called to session, the DA would walk over to them and crack a quick joke. Each time, I was surprised to see Mackey and Fourth joke back; it was as if the three of them were still backstage, waiting for their call. And then there was the judge, Thomas Reardon, trim and impeccable, who would not have been out of place in a film noir and was, in fact, a song-and-dance man—an actor, in his spare time, who'd played the male lead in local productions of *My Fair Lady*, *Guys and Dolls*, and *The Music Man*.

There was much more. And, despite the judge's best efforts, there were daily, seemingly endless, epic longueurs, which gave me more time to sit there and think of more ways in which the trial was just like a theater piece. There were so many witnesses that I lost track, and a great many pieces of evidence, some of which were bloody and difficult to look at. Through the courtroom's large windows, which faced the hills, I watched the seasons go by—saw the winter shade into spring, and then summer. And then, in the summer, I realized that all the clichéd comparisons to the theater were wrong. Three men had died. Three more were losing their freedom. The things I'd been watching could not have been much more real. When the Rats had beaten up the recycler, and run him over, on the night of their Jews versus Gentiles contest, it had happened so quickly, I'd barely registered what I had seen. In Judge Reardon's courtroom, events unfolded so slowly that it took me several months to understand that what I'd been watching was another form of violence: one that was so slow and grinding that it was almost impossible to locate in space and time. I had no doubt that the men were guilty. I'd never forget the crimes they'd committed. But, although I knew that these men had no empathy, I was surprised at how hard it was for me to let go of my own. At a remove, up on his land, hearing me describe the trial secondhand, Trevor had had no such problems. But I had spent seven months in one room with these men, and it had been a serious thing, watching the state press its full weight against those who'd threatened its monopoly on violence.

CHAPTER FIFTEEN

That fall, an encampment sprang up in City Hall Plaza. Along with sleeping tents, of which there were dozens, there was a kitchen tent (where rice was the staple, along with whatever donations came in), a library tent (filled with a random assortment of books), a tent for the camp's media center (powered by a stationary bicycle), and tents for supplies and first-aid materials. Campers strung up hand-drawn flyers that outlined Oakland's history of radical actions, paying special attention to the 1946 general strike and the Black Panthers, and detailed the ground rules that Occupy Oakland planned to abide by:

DIRECT ACTION: "Acting directly to solve problems like hunger and homelessness rather than petitioning governments for help."

EQUALITY AND CONSENSUS: "Everyone has equal voice and makes community decisions directly."

ANTICAPITALISM: "Rejecting oppressive systems and providing knowledge and resources to all, regardless of their status or ability to pay."

MUTUAL AID: "By sharing our resources and skills with each other, everyone in the community benefits."

There was a BART station at the plaza's southeast corner, and a white poster board had been fixed to the sign: "Under the BART the Beach," had been written, in blue Magic Marker, upon it.

When I first saw it, I felt as if the ghosts of Paris, 1968, had drifted across the ocean to settle.

Everyone I knew in Oakland was curious about the encampment. Occupy Wall Street had started a few weeks earlier, in New York's Zuccotti Park. Tahrir Square in Cairo had been in the headlines all year; protests there, and in Tunisia, had brought down the local regimes. In Oakland, one of the first actions that the campers took was to rechristen City Hall Plaza—henceforth to be known as "Oscar Grant Plaza"—in honor of a young black man who'd been shot in the back and killed by a BART cop who'd claimed that he'd reached for his Taser but pulled his gun out instead. And while Oakland was not Egypt or Tunisia, the expectations in Oscar Grant Plaza were high. Even Trevor, who was not politically minded, thought that the occupation would make for good spectacle. He and I went down on the camp's first day, looped around the crowded plaza together, pocketed leaflets, and talked to the campers as they pitched their tents. Trevor guessed that five hundred had gathered, or more.

"This is amazing," he said.

It was not the reaction that I had expected. I had met left-leaning Rats; ones who were pro-choice, pro–gay marriage, pro-labor; Rats who believed that income inequality had become a grave problem; that the levers of power were broken beyond repair. But I also knew that, in California, values I would have called liberal back in New York were more closely aligned with libertarianism. Neighbors I'd taken for Democrats had revealed themselves, on closer inspection, to be closet libertarians, and the few Republicans I had met had turned out to be libertarians, too. As for the techies—some of whom wanted to secede from the Union and form tax-free nation-states of their own—they really did seem to belong to the brutish cult of Ayn Rand.

"What are your politics anyway, Trevor?"

"I voted once," he replied. "Libertarian. Took the sheet to a gun shop to figure out who else to vote for."

It turned out that what Trevor meant by "amazing" was that the camp offered amazing opportunities for networking. He drummed up volunteers for the East Bay Rats' fight nights, and funneled customers off toward his bar, while I met student leaders, organizers, and gray hairs who'd come down from the Berkeley Hills or Marin. The older protesters were opposed to fracking, foreclosures, and abuses of migrant workers. The younger ones thought the whole world was insane and were all-in for all-out insurrection. One woman had made a sign that read, simply, FUCK YOU!

Eventually, the grass in the plaza died off. The ground beneath it turned muddy, and campers put down wooden pallets to walk on. On the camp's periphery, Porta-Potties, donated by Oakland's teachers' union, started to stink. But the stench mingled with the smell of burning sage and marijuana, and the overall vibe remained festive. Some of the time there was music, acoustic or amplified. In New York, the general assemblies, where group decisions were made, were held via the people's microphone. In Oakland, there was a mobile PA that got carted in and out of the plaza and was also used for improvised, plaza-wide dance parties. Zhiva's bar, Radio, was around the corner, and the Ruby Room did siphon off a few customers. But there was plenty to do in the plaza, with people arriving, on a daily basis, from Los Angeles, Portland, and other West Coast cities, from the Central Valley, and from Berkeley and San Francisco, where the occupations were smaller, more sedate affairs. Trevor came by every day, walked the perimeter, and typed names and numbers into his iPhone. For the most part, protesters were happy to see him. Perhaps they imagined a united front: the 99 percent, in tandem with the 1% bikers, fighting the 1 percent who controlled 99 percent of America's wealth. And, in fact, there was a precedent for such alliances.

In the seventies, in Europe, young people dressed in black, covered their faces, and set out for street battles with the authorities (those who had cracked down on squatters and antinuclear demonstrators in Amsterdam, Brockdorf, Hamburg, and Kreuzberg), or with fascist groups, or neo-Nazis. Some of these street fighters called themselves "Autonomen."

"What sets us apart . . . are the stones in hand and the billy clubs against our necks," a German communiqué had read. "In the tear gas clouds we feel most autonomous. What sets us apart beyond that, we do not know."

In the German media, the Autonomen were referred to as *der Schwarze Block*, or "the black bloc." They wore ski masks and scarves, hooded sweatshirts and handkerchiefs, and their avant-garde consisted of men and women in motorcycle leathers and helmets—gear that afforded the most protection in street fights. In the Netherlands, where motorcyclists were perhaps more prevalent among the Autonomen, the phrase "Black Helmet Brigade" came into play. The fact that Trevor had never heard of the Black Helmet Brigade—that he wasn't an actual, 1% biker—did not matter to the protesters.

He looked the part, and appearances mattered to the protesters, and to the city that they'd occupied.

"I was tasked with being the person to go out and engage with the Occupy folks," a city official named Arturo Sanchez would tell me. "We wanted to let them know what rules, generally, we would expect. Basically, the requests of the city were thrown to the side. But what they would have found was that there were more people, in this local government, at higher levels, who supported their overall messaging. A really strong message could have come out: in Oakland, you could have had an Occupy movement that was united with the local government."

I liked Arturo Sanchez, who was young and charismatic with a calm, compassionate manner. But I also knew that this wasn't the message the campers had gathered to send.

Down in Oscar Grant Plaza, there were committees to join, rules and hand signals to learn: jazz hands for approval; arms held up, from sternum to nose, with the palm bent down, to form a trunk, when speakers were being "irrelevant elephants." Campers gave free yoga lessons and opened a small children's village. The plaza was big—much bigger than Zuccotti Park— and the tents kept multiplying.

One day, Trevor and I arrived to find David Hilliard, the former chief of staff of the Black Panther Party, addressing the general assembly. In 1968, together with Eldridge Cleaver and several other Panthers, Hilliard had participated in the party's most radical action: an ambush of Oakland police officers, in the course of which two policemen had been wounded and the party's first and youngest recruit, Bobby Hutton, had been killed. In parts of Oakland, this made Hilliard a hero. But one of the first things Hilliard said now was that, to him, the campers in Oscar Grant Plaza look like a mess.

"In the Black Panther Party, we had our leaders," said Hilliard. "In the party, we had a ten-point plan. So, where are your leaders? What are the ten things, or eight things, or twelve you demand?"

The campers applauded politely, but this, too, was not what they'd gathered to hear. They had chosen no leaders and voiced no demands. "The Occupation is its own demand," they would say, and I think that this is why Trevor was drawn to them. Like the Rats on San Pablo, they did not explain themselves. There was nothing that they wanted, from the city or anyone else. They were simply, inexplicably, *there*. Before long, Trevor had joined a security team they had formed.

Almost from the beginning, the camp had been attracting homeless people, runaway teens, the mentally infirm or unstable—all elements that had been present in City Hall Plaza already. Early on, an unbalanced man threatened kitchen workers while holding a knife. The workers dealt with this themselves—bashed the man in the head with a two-by-four. But the need for policing, of some sort, was clear, and so, dressed in his leather jacket and vest with the EBRMC patch on the back, Trevor helped to patrol the encampment's perimeter, dropping by before his shifts at the Ruby Room and after his shifts had ended. Every once in a while some small scuffle broke out. At the general assemblies, I noticed, tempers had started to fray. Political differences among protesters started to take physical form, with older, progressive and liberal protesters sitting on the right side of the small amphitheater in front of city hall's entrance, and militants occupying the left section, which also became the smoking section. In private conversations, words like "liberal" and "progressive" were used to signify "someone too far to the right," and in public debates the phrase "Diversity of Tactics" was heard more and more often. What the phrase meant, it turned out, was that violence against property would not be condemned—although whether violence against property could properly be called "violence" remained a point of violent contention. In the meanwhile, ground rules that the camp had agreed to abide by began to exert their own influence:

"Direct Action"—the refusal to "petition governments for help."

In practice, this meant that Occupy Oakland would not ask for permission—for anything. The commitment would be to actions, not discourse.*

"Equality and Consensus"—the granting of "equal voice" and "equal powers" of decision making to each and every individual.

Among other things, this meant that city officials—who did not speak as individuals—were barred from addressing the general assemblies.

"Anticapitalism"—the rejection of "oppressive systems."

Simply put, cops were not welcome in Oscar Grant Plaza, and at first the police obliged, staying on the sidelines, standing in groups on Fourteenth Street, collecting their overtime, grumbling.

* * *

---

*There would be no talks with the city because: (1) any grievance or demand, on the part of any individual or group, might have run counter to the grievances or demands of other individuals or groups; (2) city hall was morally bankrupt and in no position to grant demands; and (3) any worthwhile demands that could have been made would have involved the dismantling of the existing political-economic order, and putting such demands forward would have been the same as asking that order to dismantle itself.

Who were the occupation's more militant elements? By and large, they were from the generations after the last peak of local struggles—not Maoists like the Panthers or Oakland's mayor, Jean Quan (although, later on, an anticolonial faction emerged), but a new wave of Communists, hostile to the socialisms of the previous century; insurrectionary anarchists, downstream from Seattle and the antiglobalization movement; and situationists ("more anarchist than the anarchists, who they find too bureaucratic," a Parisian had written in May 1968). Their political pedigrees stretched back to seventies-era Bay Area groups like No Nukes Is Not Enough Is Not Enough (a local reaction to the No Nukes Is Not Enough movement), or the Union of Concerned Commies, or to organizations that had splintered off from or formed in reaction to those groups. These people knew how to organize. They'd studied tactics and could talk just as easily about the Paris Commune as they could about Loukanikos and Kanellos, the Athenian riot dogs. They'd engaged, in the pages of literary reviews, with New York's *n + 1*, where writers still thought that the cops were potential political converts. (Anyone who'd attended ISO meetings in college knew that the army could be converted, in theory, while the cops were just there to protect property and would never come around to the people's side.) Almost without exception, they had been primed by previous actions, where the contours of their ideas and strategies had been shaped. And, in the months that followed, their arguments spilled off the pages and into the streets (which came to serve as the movement's test kitchens), before retreating to print, once again, as the moment had started to pass.

I knew that Trevor would have a hard time explaining the difference between an anarchist and an objectivist. But, time and again, I saw him drawn, as if by some internal, instinctive device, toward the militants. And though I read every leaflet handed to me, pored over communiqués, and talked to dozens of campers, I found that, more often than not, Trevor knew more than I did about the camp's actual, day-to-day workings. One night, a few weeks into the occupation, he texted and told me to meet him at work.

"You up?"

"I am now."

"Come down. They're going to evict the camp."

That evening, at the Ruby Room, two cops had come by to tell Trevor to steer clear of City Hall Plaza. He'd thought about it for just a few seconds before picking up his iPhone.

"We have to go," he'd texted.

"I'll meet you in thirty," I said.

"Make it an hour. We'll close up the bar."

Trevor was with Tyler, the Ruby Room bartender who'd fought on the side of the Gentiles on the night of the Jews versus Gentiles Fight Night. By the time the three of us got to the plaza, police had massed on the southern side of the camp. They had their riot gear on and carried tear gas and crowd-control guns. Most of them faced outward, away from the camp and toward Trevor and Tyler and me. The visors on their crowd-control helmets were up, and they were allowing those campers who wanted to exit to do so. But dozens of campers stayed where they were. Behind the police line, we watched them pick pallets up off the ground and stack them into a low barricade.

"What's going to happen?" I asked.

"Watch," Trevor said.

There were some small explosions. Bottles flew through the air. Then Trevor stepped forward, slipped past the police line, and scuttled through the barricade.

To me, he seemed like the freest of men. I knew that Trevor was a prisoner of his desires, of his habits, of his role as the captain of an organization that he was tired of but couldn't leave. To an extent, all of the East Bay Rats were slaves to their collective: as prospects, they'd been indentured servants; as Rats, they'd chained themselves to each other. Pixar Terry had told me that this was why he'd dropped out of the club: he'd put up with prospecting, but been unable to stand the thought that he'd have to support all the actions—no matter how dumb, or needlessly violent—that other Rats took. And yet, at that moment, it seemed to me that Trevor was free. My father, who was born in Russia, used to say that the writers and artists the Soviets hated the most were not anti-Soviet artists and writers (them, the Soviets had known what to do with), but a-Soviet ones: those who were not against the state but simply other, or uninterested. Trevor had that attitude toward society itself: On the one hand, he was as social as anyone I'd ever met. On the other, he was completely asocial; not in opposition to everyday rules but beyond them, or simply oblivious.

At any rate, this is what I was thinking when I noticed that Tyler was gone. I turned around and saw nothing. Then, climbing up onto a pillar, I saw that Tyler had gone in after Trevor. I stayed where I was. Police were entering the plaza. They started to dismantle the kitchen tent, then moved on to evict the campers. There was screaming and shouting, and then, from my pillar, I thought I saw Trevor, standing stock still in the middle of things. I knew that, if the roles were reversed, Trevor would have gone in to get me, just as Tyler had gone after him. As it was, Trevor had gone into the camp for no one at all, for no reason except his own curiosity.

I did not do the same for him.

It did not occur to me until well after that Trevor would have known most of the cops; that he might have been just as safe inside the camp as I was on its periphery. Instead I felt guilty and weak, standing at that slight distance, watching until the whole of the plaza was cleared. Eventually, I climbed down from the pillar, and though I stayed for an hour and saw the sun rise, I did not see Trevor or Tyler again.

That morning, I woke up worried. Trevor hadn't answered his phone or responded to texts. I couldn't find Tyler's number. Sometime after lunch I drove past the wrecked plaza and parked in front of the Ruby Room. Across the street from the bar, on the library steps, a crowd had gathered. People milled back and forth, talking about the eviction. Some were dressed all in black. Others had sticks and bandannas tied around their necks. There was no one there that I recognized. But when I knocked on the Ruby Room door, Trevor unlocked it to greet me. Nothing had happened, he told me. He'd found Tyler, and then they'd walked out—just like that—on the far side of the plaza.

"Just like that?" I asked.

Trevor shrugged and said, "Yep."

Outside, the crowd got bigger. We kept the door open and watched as it swelled and spilled into the street, then onto the sidewalk in front of the bar. After taking over the whole of the block, it began to move up Fourteenth Street, back toward Oscar Grant Plaza.

"Whose streets?"

A chant had gone up.

"Our streets!" the crowd answered in unison.

"Banks got bailed out?"

"We got sold out!"

"Ain't no party like an Oakland party?"

"'Cause an Oakland party don't stop!"

Trevor stayed at his booth in the bar, but, having done nothing that morning, I was determined to join the crowd. After a few minutes of marching, I ran into Tyler, walking the opposite way, back toward the bar, with Antonette—a punk-rock Veronica Lake who also tended bar at the Ruby Room. Antonette was close to tears. She told me she'd almost been hit, in the face, with a tear-gas canister.

"Be careful," she said as I left them.

Outside the plaza, there were more cops than I could count: Oakland cops, and many more from surrounding cities. Oddly, the police used the same formulation—"Mutual Aid"—that the campers did: "The City of Oakland appreciates the outstanding mutual aid assistance provided by local law enforcement agencies," city officials would say. "Mutual aid was provided by the cities of Alameda, Berkeley, Emeryville, Fremont, Hayward, Newark, Pleasanton, San Jose, San Leandro, and Union City, as well as the Alameda County Sheriff's Department, San Francisco County Sheriff's Department, Santa Clara County Sheriff's Department, the California Highway Patrol, the Solano County Sheriff's Department, and the University of California Police Department." Even in New York, with its police force the size of a standing army, I'd never seen so many cops in one place. The cordon they'd formed stretched all the way across Fourteenth Street and on the front line the police stood in formation, stone-faced, as protesters did their best to cajole them, shame them, insult them, or prod them into some sort of action.

They took a lot of abuse. Some were covered in paint that protesters had thrown, and, several times, they did take action, firing tear-gas rounds above the protesters, who would run, with white chemical smoke wafting after. When the smoke cleared the crowd reassembled—and, I noticed, not everyone ran. Once in a while, I'd see a protester in a bandanna pick a tear-gas canister up off the ground and lob it back toward the cops. At one point, I saw two men in uniform, standing stock-still with a flag that said: IRAQ VETERANS FOR PEACE. One was a sailor, the other one a marine. They stood at attention, some yards from the cordon, and remained motionless during the sallies. A rhythm established itself: tear-gas guns, like snare drums, a running away, and then the drift back toward the plaza. During one of the lulls, a cop raised his crowd-control rifle and shot the marine in the head.

"In the Marine Corps, I was a tactical systems administrator, doing IT work," the marine would tell me, once he'd taught himself to talk again. His name was Scott Olsen. A sweet, skinny kid in his early twenties, he had long, frizzy hair and a fractured skull that had only just started to heal. "I was in an infantry battalion, so we deployed to Iraq," he said. "To Al-Qa'im, Iraq, in 2006. We were extended for the surge, and got back in April 2007. Less than a year later I went back, to Haditha Dam, in Iraq, and stayed there until September 2008."

Back in the States, Olsen had gotten a tech job in San Francisco. In his off-hours, he'd been a regular at Occupy San Francisco—that encampment was near his office—and he'd been walking toward it when Occupy Oakland issued a call for support. Seeing it on Twitter, Olsen had switched directions and taken BART into Oakland.

"As soon as I got to Fourteenth and Broadway, I saw the police, and lots of demonstrators," said Olsen. "I joined the crowd. Up front, I saw a 'Veterans for Peace' flag. I knew that I probably knew the guy with it, so I went up there, and we were standing there, in the gap in between the protesters and the police. People were surrounding us, taking pictures. It's a very surreal experience, to be facing down against the police—to be in that position. After the police started to attack us and use tear gas against us, I was shot in the head by a direct-stabilized beanbag round. I woke up on the ground after I was hit. I must have gone out for a few seconds, but I woke and there were people trying to help me. I didn't realize how hurt I'd become.

I thought it was just a minor injury. I wanted them to leave me alone. But as soon as they started asking my name, and I couldn't muster up an answer, I knew that I should let them help me. They put me in their car and took me to Highland Hospital.

"When you dress up like a soldier," said Olsen, "when you train with soldiers, and when you have the weapons of soldiers, you think you are a soldier, and you want to hurt somebody. That shouldn't be in Oakland. Combat should not take place here. It's one thing to experience it in a war-torn country. It's something else to see it here."

CHAPTER SIXTEEN

A chain-link fence had gone up around Oscar Grant Plaza, and when I arrived, I found that a crowd had gathered again. By now, we'd all seen footage of Scott Olsen's injury, which had occurred the night before. In the immediate aftermath, a small group of campers had rushed up to help. They'd formed a circle around the marine, started to pick him up off the pavement. Right at that moment, a cop had tossed a flash-bang grenade at their feet. We'd all seen footage of that as well. Less than twenty-four hours had passed since then—the mood was dark—and I was relieved to see Trevor, standing up against the fence.

"What's up?" he said when he saw me.

"This fence," I said. "It wasn't here yesterday."

"This fence?"

With both of his hands on the chain-link, Trevor gave the fence a good shove.

"Doesn't feel sturdy to me."

He began to rock the fence, gently, back and forth on its

foundation. A few people gathered around him to watch. A few more came up beside him and put their own hands on the fence. Trevor seemed not to notice. A look of concentration had come over his face: it was as if he were solving some sort of math problem.

"Fuck it," he said, and shoved with his shoulder.

The fence came down. The crowd rushed into the plaza. But the plaza was empty now, and a moment later the crowd rushed back out and onto the sidewalk by the BART station where Trevor and I were standing. Just a few cops were leaning, outside of their cars, on the far side of Fourteenth Street. They did not move, but everyone on our side of the street was restless, and no one seemed to know what the next step would be. I looked up at Trevor, who looked down at me. Then I watched him step off the sidewalk and into the street, raise his right arm, and shout: "Take the intersection!"

Immediately, the crowd rushed into the intersection, filling it from corner to corner and chanting:

"Whose streets?"

"Our streets!"

After a few rounds of chanting an order was given, and repeated via people's microphone, and the crowd began to march, heading south, toward OPD headquarters.

I looked at Trevor again and, for the first time since I'd met him, saw him grinning from ear to ear.

"Are you proud of yourself?" I asked.

Trevor gave it a few seconds' thought as we walked.

"Yep," he said. "Want to go to Radio?"

"Don't you want to go on the march?"

"Don't care about the march."

He turned the corner and glanced back to see if I'd followed.

"I don't care about the politics," he said. "I'm only here for the violence."

* * *

Oakland's mayor, Jean Quan, was new on the job, and unsure of her role in the proceedings. The city's police chief, Anthony Batts, had quit his job on the very day that the first tents had gone up in City Hall Plaza. His resignation had been followed by others. And if Quan found herself isolated and overwhelmed, she was also unprepared, ideologically, to deal with the protesters.

As a student at Berkeley in the sixties, Quan had joined the Maoist Third World Liberation Front in a long, bloody strike on behalf of minority students, which had succeeded—despite Ronald Reagan, who'd sent in the National Guard—in forcing the school to set up an ethnic studies program. Back then, Quan had worked with Richard Aoki, a Black Panther field marshal who was later found out to have been an informant for the FBI. Forty years later, as a member of Oakland's city council, she'd joined a human chain separating OPD officers from activists at an Oscar Grant protest; it was something that the cops had never forgiven her for. In New York, Mike Bloomberg had cracked down, a few times, on Zuccotti Park; there, protesters had been maced and beaten and arrested by the hundreds. But in Oakland, the mayor, who still presented herself as a radical, had done her best to align her interests with those of the campers (why couldn't they be more like she'd been? she'd ask) and, until the eviction, a semblance of order had been maintained.

After the eviction, all bets were called off. Mayor Quan let it be known that the campers were welcome back in the plaza, and invited a contingent of liberal, progressive activists to set up an alternate campsite in a tiny park, called Snow Park, by Lake Merritt. The police were incredulous: the mayor might as well have raised a white flag. But, given the absence of

Anthony Batts, it was hard for the campers to tell if anyone at all was in charge of the police department. That evening, they reoccupied the plaza.

This occupation—the second—was not the same as the first. There was less sage now, less incense, more marijuana smoke. There were more runaways, too, more homeless people and addicts. Online, you could buy a gay porno that someone had shot in the tents: "Occupy Your Throat," it was called.

At the general assembly, there was talk of a general strike. Given the provisions against sympathy strikers, as set forth in Taft-Hartley, it was hard to know what a modern-day general strike would have looked like. But the measure that called for one was voted in, along with a resolution that called for the respect of Diversity of Tactics. Old debates about violence resurfaced: compared to the violence of gentrification, the violence of the media, the violence of capitalism itself, who cared about broken windows and burning cop cars? Walking through the camp, I'd hear the words "smashy, smashy." And, at the same time, the camp itself became more violent. There were fistfights and robberies, rumors of sexual assaults. Trevor stuck with the security squad. The cops remained at their distance. On some nights, it felt as though Oakland had shown up to occupy Occupy Oakland.

On October 28, the first full day after the plaza's reoccupation, pro-democracy demonstrators marched to the US embassy in Cairo to voice their solidarity with Occupy Oakland. On October 30, I flew to New York: my friend John Barr had gotten leave from his posting as an army medic in Afghanistan and was spending a few days in the city. On the evening of November 2, I went online to see how the general strike in Oakland had gone.

Tens of thousands of people had turned out. Starting from Oscar Grant Plaza, they had marched, en masse, down the highway toward Oakland's port—which they had shut down for several hours. It was not a general strike in the strict sense of the term; not all of Oakland's unions had been involved. But it was the biggest mass action that Oakland had seen since the general strike of 1946; people in other West Coast port cities had marched in solidarity, and, on Facebook and Twitter, neighbors of mine—men and women who'd never brought politics up in my company—were calling it the most inspiring day of their lives.

Afterward, there was another action. One block away from Oscar Grant Plaza, protesters took the old Travelers Aid Society building—a vacant two-story building midway between Latham Square and the plaza—and claimed it for the occupation. On the Livestreams, I watched cameras pan over the barricade. Occupiers were inside the building already. Across all the windows, they'd unfurled a banner that read: OCCUPY EVERYTHING. Then, the police moved in.

Fires burned. Tear gas was deployed, and beanbag rounds were fired. A protester panned his camera across the police line. "Is this okay?" he asked. "Is this okay?" Without giving a warning, one cop raised his crowd-control rifle and fired.

Later that night, a friend of Trevor's, who'd been a ranger in the army and had served in Iraq and Afghanistan, found himself in front of a group of riot cops.

"Move," they instructed. "Move! Move! Move!"

Trevor's friend didn't move quickly enough. Instead, he saluted, began to walk backward, and, as the cops prodded with their batons, said, "I want you to know, man, I killed for my country."

The police piled on and beat him severely, rupturing the ranger's spleen.

* * *

"Why don't they occupy Piedmont?" people asked in the weeks that followed. "Why don't they go to San Francisco—which has an actual stock exchange?"

The media were in no position to explain. The *Oakland Tribune* had been bought, several times, since William Knowland's suicide: no longer housed in the Tribune Tower (which had been flipped, with money raised from Chinese businessmen via a government program that granted fast-track green cards to foreign investors, and was being turned into a near-sourcing call center), the *Tribune* was now part of the Bay Area News Group, which was owned by an umbrella company that specialized in buying regional papers, gutting them, and combining their editorial operations. That company was owned, in turn, by a hedge fund, which was owned by another hedge fund—the higher you looked, the less transparency and accountability there seemed to be. At the same time, Quan did her best to avoid journalists, most of the campers refused to talk to the mainstream media (though a few were happy to talk to RT, the Russian news station, which had seized upon Occupy Oakland as a prime piece of anti-American propaganda), and it was all that reporters could do to keep up with the news cycle, which was moving now at the speed of tweets, Instagrams, Livestreams, and T1 connections. There was no one to explain that the Occupy movement—the form it had taken in Oakland, at least—aimed at insurrection rather than reform; that, for better or worse, this is what the revolution looked like, right now, in America. And if the local media were nearing collapse, the plaza was also looking worse for wear.

When I got back from New York, the runaways were still there, along with the homeless people and addicts, and they'd been joined by groups of teenagers, or men in their early twenties, who rode around on dirt bikes, pushed others out of the way, and panhandled, aggressively, in ways that could have been mistaken for muggings. Trevor seemed wary now, and suggested that we go shopping at the Army Navy Store. At the first one we tried, we found that there'd been a run on gas masks. At the second one, I bought an elegant Israeli gas mask. At the third, Trevor got one, made in eastern Europe, that looked like a prop from *Mad Max*. Then we went back to old rhythms: gas by the plaza and around the corner to Radio, which Zhiva had turned into a medical station, with bandages and Mylanta, for tear-gas burns, stocked behind the bar. One thing I remember about this time is the smell of tear gas, and the vinegar protesters used to soak their bandannas ahead of tear-gas attacks: combined, they made Oakland's downtown smell like a darkroom. Another thing I remember is that, by the BART station, a masked figure walked past three Oakland cops and me. He dragged a broom handle behind him, at the end of which he'd tied a claw hammer. Scraped across the pavement, it was the single most frightening thing I'd seen in Oakland: a tool for breaking bank windows, or people who got in the way. The police ignored it. But that night, at home, as I hung my gas mask up, like a suit jacket, I said to Lucy: "I hope that no one gets killed in the plaza tomorrow."

The next day, somebody was killed.

It happened at the very end of a workday, on the day of Occupy Oakland's two-month anniversary. The plaza was crowded—more so than it had been all week—and I was on foot, walking past the city hall building, when I heard what sounded like fireworks.

I'd learned, by now, from time spent with Trevor, that, in real life, fireworks often sound like gunshots, while actual gunshots sound, quite a bit, like fireworks. Still, it took a moment to understand why everyone else in the plaza had begun to sprint, quietly, past me.

"Oh, fuck," I heard as somebody went by.

"For real?"

"It's on now!"

By the time I got down to the BART station entrance, most of the campers had scattered. There were a few dozen left, along with the ever-present young thugs, still circling around us on dirt bikes. On the ground in front of us there was a young man—a teenager, I guessed—who'd been shot in the head. There was blood, and brain matter, and without talking about it, a group of us formed a circle to keep the gawkers and TV news crews from sticking cameras in the dead man's face.

His name, I found out, was Kayode Ola Foster. He was twenty-five and had been staying in Oscar Grant Plaza for just a few days. His death seemed to be the result of a dime-bag drug deal gone wrong. Campers argued that the shooting had nothing to do with the camp. In Oakland, they said, murders like this happened all the time. And while it seemed that the killing had *something* to do with the camp, they were right in that nothing about it was all that unusual. This was confirmed, that night in the plaza, by a man I met named Coach Todd Walker. Walker looked more than a bit like Ving Rhames. A middle-aged guy who worked for funeral parlors in Oakland, he spent his off-hours volunteering with kids in the city. In the past, Walker told me, he'd taken his kids to the morgue to see the bodies laid out on the tables. He'd walk them through the embalming process, put them in caskets and close the lid, tell them that this was how some stories ended. Then, he told me, he'd had to stop: kids he'd mentored had begun to show up on the tables. As we parted, Coach Walker handed me his business card, with his name and an inspirational message: "It's about saving the kids." Above it, he'd printed the name of his organization—Restoring Inner-City Peace—and the organization's acronym: R.I.P.

There were moments of reprieve. Early one morning, following a protest and the police action that the protest provoked, there was a wedding by the BART station entrance. The "Under the BART the Beach" sign was long gone. But, once again, the mood had turned festive.

"Bakesale," the bride said, "in my heart of hearts, I am committing myself to you in the movement in true dedication to social change."

"Um," the groom said. "Amanda Hugginchicken: you are the most amazing person I ever met. Together, we will take this movement everywhere that peace should ring, and I can't wait to stand with you on that shore, look at what we did, and bask in that love."

"By the power that's in me for the whole damn universe," said the camp cleric, "I now pronounce you man and wife, or something like that."

"They're tearing down the tents!" a member of the wedding party shouted.

"Let's protest!" someone else said, and a third person said, "It's okay. They'll be back in a couple of days!"

In fact, the camp was not allowed to reestablish itself. Occupy Oakland was still in the headlines; in the *New York Times*, stories appeared on a regular basis. But most of the people I knew in Oakland had lost patience with Occupy. The sing-alongs had stopped. There were no more fruit baskets sent down by Chez Panisse in Berkeley. The liberals and the progressives had wandered away, though others streamed slowly into the city, squatting in old buildings and showing up for what came to be called the "Fuck the Police March and

Demonstration"—an event that took place on Saturday nights and was referred to, informally, as "taking the pigs for a walk." On San Pablo, quite close to the East Bay Rats clubhouse, a group of anarchists tried to raise rabbits, gave up, and released the animals, and for a few weeks that followed, bunnies could be seen hopping along the avenue.

"Look," I said to Trevor one day. "There's a rabbit. Go get one!"

Just a few months had gone by. But by that point, the Black Muslim murder trial might as well have happened in another century.

Periodically, Trevor would ask me if I had found what I'd expected to find in Oakland. Was he what I'd expected? Were the Rats? What were the things that had made the strongest impressions?

I thought about Sam and his wrestlers; the drama with J.J.; the fights and the fight nights and that one recycler I could have helped. But the two things I mentioned to Trevor involved Occupy Oakland. One was an ill-fated attempt, on the part of the occupation, to take over Oakland Auditorium. The other involved the East Bay Rats' flag, which was now flying proudly over OPD headquarters.

We'd known about the building takeover for weeks—the when and how of it, if not quite the target. But in retrospect it had been obvious. The Oakland Auditorium was within walking distance of city hall. It was big enough to accommodate the entire occupation. And then, there was the symbolic import: Oakland's meeting place and social center, abandoned years earlier, fenced off and vacant, unused. On January 28 (a day still remembered, in certain quarters, as "Move-In Day," or the day of "The Battle of Oakland"), demonstrators gathered again in

Oscar Grant Plaza. "It's cold outside," a flyer read. "Like millions of people in this country Occupy Oakland has no home. And yet, all over the city, thousands of buildings stand empty. On January 28, we're going to occupy one of those buildings and turn it into a social center. We're going to fill the space with a kitchen, first aid station, sleeping quarters and an assembly area, libraries and free school classes, as well as hundreds of uses yet to be determined. Let's establish our new home, defend it, and adapt it to Oakland's needs. *We get what we can take*."

There was a sound truck, and a marching band in the plaza. Lucy was with me, and we saw protesters who had brought shields, made from rubber lids from garbage cans, on which they had painted either anarchy symbols or peace signs. One demonstrator had brought a stuffed armchair, which he would carry throughout the day and crouch behind during scuffles with cops: he was Occupy Oakland's idea of an armchair warrior. Off to the side, a phalanx of protesters stood behind movable barricades fashioned out of large sheets of corrugated metal. On one of the sheets, in red and black letters, they had written: COPS MOVE OUT. The other sheet read: COMMUNE MOVE IN.

There were hundreds, if not thousands, of demonstrators. The band started up, and the sound truck. We began to march, winding our way through downtown and Chinatown. There were very few cops, and nothing slowed our progress as we approached Laney, a community college by the Lake Merritt BART station.

It was a small campus; the auditorium was just a few blocks away. But Laney had been built in the wake of the student unrest of the sixties. It was "riot proof"—which is to say, it had been built to splinter crowds of protesters. And, like the sixties themselves, our crowd had splintered and lost its momentum as people stopped to talk, or smoke, or wander, lost, past the brutalist buildings. When we emerged, finally, on the far side of the campus, we saw that the cops were there, after all, waiting for us inside and around the auditorium itself.

Explosions followed. Crowd-control missiles were fired at the protesters, who replied with projectiles of their own. Lucy and I ducked into the Oakland Museum next door. But the museum was another brutalist building, open on all sides to the outside, and when the tear gas started, those of us inside the museum were gassed as well. From the steps, Lucy and I watched the phalanx fall back, behind its large metal shields, regroup, and advance, in formation, on the police. Miraculously (this is what I brought up with Trevor, and something I'd never expected to see), the police retreated. But the battle didn't last long, or end well for the protesters, and later that night, hundreds were arrested in a dragnet the police had set up in front of the downtown YMCA. Some escaped into the building and out through the back. One went up to the third floor, stripped off his shirt, sat down, and began to pretend to work out.

Timmers, the Rat, happened to be sitting on the next bench, well into his daily workout.

"Fuck that," is what Timmers had thought. Weeks later, he told me that he'd gotten up, called out to the cops, and turned the kid in. "He might have been crying. I didn't feel bad. Then I walked downstairs—the cops had some Occupy types on their stomachs, out on the street. I might have kicked a few on my way out."

That same night, protesters got into city hall and knocked over a vitrine with an architect's model of city hall—another image that sticks in my mind, along with a sense of what Oakland's streets would have looked like, to strangers, that day. From certain angles, they really had looked like a battle-ground:

And yet, when you pulled back, just so, you saw that the battle took up just one block, while groups of Chinatown residents stood nearby, watching, from what seemed, to them, to be a safe distance.

Thinking of that day today, I'm reminded of J.J.'s predicament, vis-à-vis the Rats and Norton Aaron's death: there, a murder mystery hadn't been solved, because it had been in no one's interest to solve it. Here, a battle scene altered its shape, became more interesting and complicated once you'd zoomed out away from it. But it had been in no one's interest to zoom away, explain the difference between street fights and street theater, or argue that, perhaps, in the here and now, there was no difference between them at all—and that, in fact, there never had been.

"You mentioned two things," said Trevor. "Two things that made an impression?"

"The 'Fuck the Police March and Demonstrations,'" I said.

"The ones that took place every Saturday night? They were a lot less violent than anyone expected them to be."

"They weren't really violent at all. But do you remember the first?"

"On New Year's Night?"

"That one. Demonstrators pulled the flag down from a flag-pole in front of OPD headquarters."

"They pulled the American flag down and burned it."

"They did," I said. "The next day, a bunch of Rats pulled up in front of OPD headquarters. The demonstrators had gathered again, and the cops were all dressed in their riot gear. The Rats rode up on the sidewalk between them, and John Firpo put his hand into Dave LaBree's knapsack—the cops got nervous, seeing him do that. Then Firpo pulled out an American flag."

"The flag Biker Mike brought back from Vietnam. We used it for Norton's funeral."

"The cops took it, raised it, and thanked you."

"Yep," Trevor said. "It's flying there now, like a pirate flag over the city. Did I ever show you the note that we got?"

"What note?"

"The one that we got from the cops."

Trevor pulled out his iPhone, scrolled through the photos, and showed me one of a letter, on OPD stationery. "Dear East Bay Rats Motorcycle Club," it began.

The Oakland Police Department would like to thank you for your generous donation of the American Flag which we intend to hang in front of our Police Administration Building located at 455–7th Street.

On behalf of the Oakland Police Department and the members we proudly serve, we thank you and are forever grateful and humbled by your selfless act of kindness.

Sincerely,
Howard A. Jordan
[Interim] Chief of Police

EPILOGUE

We'd come to stay for a year. But California is a land of lotus-eaters, and we'd become lotus-eaters ourselves. We loved our home and the friends we had made. We'd learned to love Oakland, and watched as it changed, although now it seemed to be changing too quickly. After San Francisco, Oakland had become the most rapidly gentrifying city in America. Rents were doubling, then tripling, all around us. Home prices increased by 20 or 30 percent every year. At open houses, those who expected to pay asking prices, or top them, were outbid by flippers who'd pay much more, in cash, on the spot. The result was a tidal wave of displacement, which Trevor summed up perfectly when he told me, "Oakland is getting much nicer. But if keeps getting nicer, we'll all have to leave."

And yet, Oakland did not become safer. The murder rate remained high, the clearance rates remained low, and in 2012 Oakland became the nation's "robbery capital" (according to what was left of the *Oakland Tribune*), with more robberies per capita than in any other American city.* At the Oakland Museum, a gold rush exhibit was broken into, twice, in short order; down the street from our home, the Temescal branch of the Bank of the West was held up five times in the course of five weeks; and, after a series of BART station muggings, our neighbors on Rockridge pooled money online and hired a private police force. I kept tabs on Anthony Batts, who'd moved on to the Kennedy School at Harvard and then become the police commissioner for Baltimore (a job he would lose in the wake of the Baltimore riots of 2015), while in Oakland, Jean Quan went through three police chiefs in the course of a single week.

The following year—our third in Oakland—Trevor quit drinking, not for the first time, but this time for good. Then he met a woman named Jordan, who was smart, young, and beautiful, and who had even more tattoos than Trevor did. Before long they were living together: for the first time in ages, the rest of the Rats had the clubhouse all to themselves. Almost immediately, the club began to attract new prospects, most of whom seemed to be veterans of the wars in Iraq and Afghanistan. I still knew all the old faces, but these prospects were surly, unfriendly, and I didn't get to know any of them. Then I got married, in Tucson, where Lucy's family was, and Trevor and Jordan came out for the wedding, driving through Joshua Tree in a truck that Trevor had bought with money he'd inherited from his grandmother. Days later, during our honeymoon in the Four Corners, my phone buzzed. "Jordan's pregnant," Trevor had texted. "You'll teach your kids about writing and music, and I'll teach mine how to kill."

He knew me well enough, by now, to know that I'd know that he was only half kidding.

---

*In Cleveland, the second-place city, the robbery rate was 36 percent lower.

Soon he was married. Biker Mike performed the ceremony and at the reception, in a Berkeley hofbrau, Jason Lockwood welcomed Jordan into the fold. "I wanted to take a moment," he said, "to welcome Jordan into our chosen family, one that has started, more and more, to resemble the traditional meaning of that word."

Afterward, I asked him: If Trevor retired, would he consider taking his place?

"I wouldn't," said Jason. "The joke that I've made is that I'd turn us into a knitting club. I might do an interim thing, if needed. But, honestly, I'm too timid. There's guys in the club who could maintain the spirit and not go Bonzo at the same time. I'm not one of them."

For Jason, the choices came down to Kaj—a Rat who'd known Trevor for ages—and a Rat named Englebert, who was married, had kids, and did not come around all that often. "Kaj's a good balance of tough guy, blue-collar, and at-home, custom-motorcycle builder," said Jason. "In short, he'd make a good prez. Englebert is a Harley mechanic, and has been, locally, for a long time. He knows everyone from every MC across the Bay and is on good terms with all of them. I think he'd just naturally drift us in their direction. It wouldn't be placid. But, certainly, we'd have less of a *Road Warrior* vibe."

"And when everyone gets married," I asked. "When everyone gets settled, and old . . ."

I couldn't quite phrase the question.

"Well, here's the thing," Jason said. "We've always done a good job of cruising the line. We're not outlaws, or 1%-ers. Then again, we're not the AMA. What we excel at is the stupid stuff. The cops always chuckle when they bust up our parties because something ridiculous, but not quite illegal, is happening when they show up. The short answer to what I think you're trying to ask is yes, we do want to have our cakes and eat them. We want to break laws, but just to act dumb and to do stupid stuff. The truth is, we're kind of lazy."

"Except when it comes to burning things."

"That doesn't take energy. That just takes gas."

Trevor moved out of Oakland and settled nearby, in Emeryville. He got a job as an irrigation worker for the City of Albany; outdoor work, with good benefits and the option of sending his children to Albany's excellent schools. He bought a Harley-Davidson—a purple one, with a built-in CD player, that had been owned by a black guy—but held on to his position as the club's president. Then, a few months after the birth of Trevor's son, Mason, Lucy and I moved back to New York, where we stayed for six months while Lucy taught a few classes. When she was through, we drove back to the East Bay, where we stayed for another six months. In the end, finding that Oakland had become too expensive for us, we moved back to New York for good.

All in all, we crisscrossed the country three times, taking a southern route, through New Orleans and Texas, a northern route, through the Dakotas, and a middle way, which led through Chicago. Wherever we went, we saw the same places: the same farmers' markets, artisanal boutiques, and retro-futuristic cocktail bars where the exposed pipes and Edison lightbulbs spoke to steampunk's strange nostalgia for a world in which actual people made actual things. Everywhere we looked, there was a fetishistic attention to detail—as if the micro-decisions we could make now, as consumers, could ward off the sense that our slide toward a place in the service economy was, in some sense, a choice we had all made.

During my last months in Oakland, I'd driven around East Oakland, searching in vain (I thought) for the scrap yard that Abdo S. Allen—the man who had owned the tank that had torn down West Oakland—had owned. And then, at a scrap yard by the Oakland Airport, in a deep, industrial corner of the city, I had found Allen's son, Charlie.

Charlie Allen remembered the tank very well; he himself had driven it on occasion. He told me about his drinking days, which he'd spent in the ruins of the same neighborhoods that had been cleared by the tank. He told me about his father's days as a race-car driver and showed me his scrap yard, where much of San Francisco's architectural history, and much of Oakland's, lay in wait for reclamation. Now that he himself is in his late sixties, Charlie was hoping to sell the scrap yard and liquidate all that this family had liquidated. As he talked, it occurred to me that Charlie's father would have loved the Rats. They were gear heads, too, mechanics and machinists as well as destroyers. Any one of them would have given a week of his life for a few moments behind the controls of Abdo Allen's tank.

I had driven around West Oakland, as well, sometimes passing the Oakland Auditorium (soon to be converted into tech offices, I had heard), visiting friends I had made, looking at all the old houses and parks. San Francisco, with its creatives, curators, makers, and disruptors, was just across the Bay, and houses in the Lower Bottoms were now being bought and converted—quietly, from the inside out—by those who imagined whole new neighborhoods where these very old neighborhoods had once been. The city's future was here, but I wouldn't be around to see it.

All of the while, I was counting the days until Lucy and I hit the road one last time. We really had grown to love Oakland, though the things we loved most were also the things that were disappearing. New York was still our home. We put the top down and drove.

CODA

Alex Abramovich: So, you were saying—your dad grew up in West Oakland?

Charlie Allen: Yes, he went to McClymonds High School. I believe, in the thirties, my grandparents started having grocery stores in Oakland.

AA: Do you recall where they were?

CA: We actually demolished the last store they had. There was a house above the store, and they lived in that, until, for redevelopment, we tore the house down. That was my grandparents' house. The house on the other side of the family—we tore that down, too.

AA: Were the grandparents still living when you did that?

CA: My grandmother was in the state hospital and my grandfather, he'd passed away.

AA: What did your grandfather do before he ran grocery stores?

CA: He came from Lebanon and was a merchant. He used to pack clothes and pots and pans on his back and go up into the lumber camps in northern California. My father had four brothers, and they were all raised working in the grocery stores. Then, down the road, he had a sister who married a fellow and they had a clothing store in the Dimond District of Oakland. Back then, braseros would come from Mexico, to work in the summer. He had a truck and would sell them clothes. They would buy shirts or pants, just to cash their checks. He carried a lot of cash and cashed their paychecks. In the summertime, I used to go out with him and help.

AA: How did your father, Abdo, get involved with demolition?

CA: You know, he was into race cars. He had his own racetrack, Capitol Speedway, in West Sacramento. They used to have a building, right where Laney College is now, called the Acquisition Building—the Oakland Auditorium was right across the street. It was a big metal building and he was one of the founders. They had indoor midget car racing. Nowadays, environmentally, there's no way you could do that. You'd come out of there covered in rubber and smoke. But they used to have midget car racing six nights a week around here. Then, when he got out of racing—he just all of the sudden quit it, sold the track—he went to work for somebody who was in the demolition business. He got his own license. And he wouldn't even talk about racing. I guess it's like people who were in a war. He lost a lot of friends to racing. In those days, guys was getting killed all the time.

AA: It was a good time to get into demolition in Oakland?

CA: In the sixties? Oh yeah, there was lots of stuff to tear down. [Looks over at photos on the wall.] That's me, there. Have you heard of Playland at the Beach? It was in San Francisco.

I tore that down almost by myself. Over here, on Sansome and Lombard? That was right after we did Playland. There were two six-story icehouses. It's all large buildings now, right off the Embarcadero, but there were these big icehouses then. At the time, we thought it was amazing—it was the end of Vietnam, 1973, and steel went to a hundred dollars a ton, and copper was a dollar a pound. We thought that was unbelievable.

AA: Would you bring the tank out to all of these projects?

CA: No. The tank was really mainly used for publicity.

AA: What I've read is that it plowed through Victorians more quickly than anything else could.

CA: Well, that is true. It just ran through them. I took down, probably, two hundred houses in West Oakland, when redevelopment went through. At the time, you know, they didn't have communication. We'd get stuck in basements. This photograph—there were blocks of housing, where the post office now is. That's where we used it. But, you know, you couldn't load it or anything. The last time he used it was to tear down a dairy farm. He ran it through a big barn, but a big timber pushed right through and hit him in the shoulder. He was a daredevil type of guy. That's his car-racing helmet, and goggles, over there.

AA: It sounds like your family had a lot to do with tearing down the Oakland that you'd grown up in.

CA: We sure did. I actually ended up tearing down Oakland High School, where I went. We tore down Prescott Jr. High, too. Like I said, we wrecked our grandparents' houses. There's areas where we just took down—you know, the shopping center, as you come off the freeway on Adeline? There's a big shopping center there now? That was houses.

AA: Were there things there that you were sorry to take down?

CA: No, because no one saved anything then. Times changed just as quickly. People say, "Oh, you tore down those Victorians!" Nobody wanted them. My grandparents got ten thousand dollars or less for their house. Nobody wanted those houses.

ACKNOWLEDGMENTS

Thanks to Dorothy Lazard and the staff of the Oakland History Room, and to Betty Marvin and Gail Lombardi at the Oakland Cultural Heritage Survey. Thanks to Sasha Archibald, Stijn Schiffeleers, and Claire Ball at the Oakland Standard. Thanks to Jeff Norman, Kathy Geritz, and Michael Glawogger.

Thanks to Gifford Hartmann and Lawrence Jarach. Thanks to Rick Prelinger, Wade Wright, Max Allstadt, John Russo, Thomas Peele, and Susie Cagle.

Thanks to all of the Rats, ex-Rats, and associates who are named in this book and were unfailingly generous with their time, thoughts, and friendship. Thanks to several Rats not named in this book: Charlie Hewett, Jerry Osborne, and others who know who they are.

Thanks to Tyler Hutton.

Thanks to Trevor's family—his father, Stuart—and my own dad. Thanks to Jordan Latham, Lauren Lockwood, and the rest of the women who've learned to live with the Rats.

Thanks to Cecily Reynolds.

Thanks to Jim Saleda and Jason England.

Thanks to Yakpasua Zazaboi and Clem Daniels.

Thanks to Sam Khandaghabadi.

Thanks to Boots Riley, Harvey Stafford, the gang at Moe's Books, and Leo Ritz-Barr.

Thanks to Charlie Allen, Scott Olsen, and Vince Passaro.

Thanks to Joshua Clover.

Thanks to John and Nina Zurier, Pamela Wylson-Ryckman, Thomas Ryckman, Trevor Paglen, Anne Walsh, Chris Kubick, Moriah Ulinskas, Dominic Willsdon, Sean Uyehara, Phil and Jules Tippett, and Dan and Erika Clowes.

Thanks to the Knowles/Fischer clan—David, Jennifer, Eli, and Mira—for the soft landing, good music, great dinners, and excellent company.

Thanks to Cristina Mueller and Olive Beatrix Faust Nosowsky.

Thanks to friends who read the manuscript: Dan Halpern, Aaron Retica, Michael Miller, Sam Lipsyte, Ceridwen Morris, Thomas Jones, Jenny Offill, and Chris Sorrentino. Words can't express my debt to Ethan Nosowsky.

Thanks to John Barr, Christina Lewis-Halpern, and Andrew Gillings.

Thanks to my second dad, Bruce Diones.

Thanks to Jerry Smith and Buzz Buzzelli, who interviewed Gus De Serpa in 1997. Thanks to Chris Thompson, Jonathan Lethem, Robert Gordon, Nat Rich, Naomi Wax, and Bill Shapiro.

Thanks to Ariel Kaminer, Joel Lovell (who put my hospital bills on his personal credit card), and Andrew Hetherington.

Thanks to Gillian Blake, Eleanor Embry, and the rest of the team at Henry Holt.

Thanks to Elyse Cheney, Alex Jacobs, Adam Eaglin, Sam Freilich, Hannah Elnan, and Sarah Rainone at Cheney Literary.

Profound thanks to the Goldstines, especially Danny and Hilary, for their friendship and kindness, and for providing a home away from home.

Thanks, most of all, to Doug Jaffe.

ILLUSTRATION CREDITS

ABOUT THE AUTHOR

ALEX ABRAMOVICH has taught at the New School, worked for *The New Yorker* and *Feed*, and written for *The New York Times*, the *London Review of Books*, and many other publications. He was born in Moscow and lives in Astoria, Queens.